EASY PIANO

SONGS FROM AND INSPIRED
BY THE HIT TV SERIES

W9-BAH-271

ISBN-13: 978-1-4234-5481-6
ISBN-10: 1-4234-5481-2

Disney characters and artwork © Disney Enterprises, Inc.

WALT DISNEY MUSIC COMPANY

DISTRIBUTED BY

HAL•LEONARD®
CORPORATION

7777 W. BLUEMOUND RD. P.O. BOX 13819 MILWAUKEE, WI 53213

In Australia Contact:
Hal Leonard Australia Pty. Ltd.
4 Lentara Court
Cheltenham, Victoria, 3192 Australia
Email: ausadmin@halleonard.com.au

Visit Hal Leonard Online at
www.halleonard.com

THE BEST OF BOTH WORLDS

Words and Music by MATTHEW GERRARD
and ROBBIE NEVIL

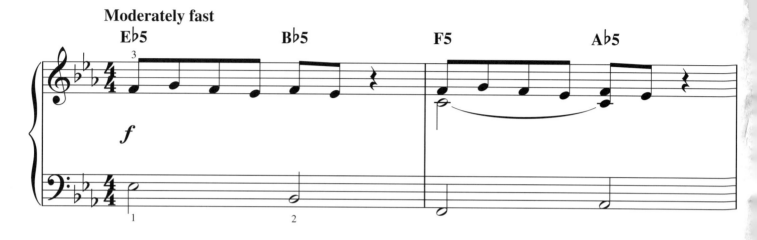

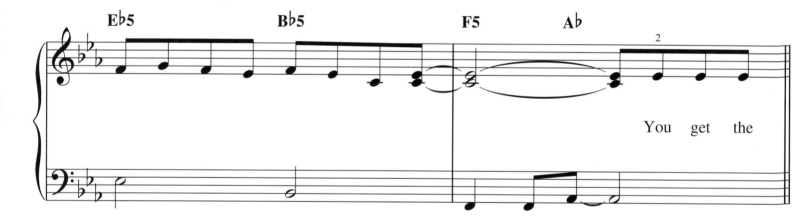

You get the

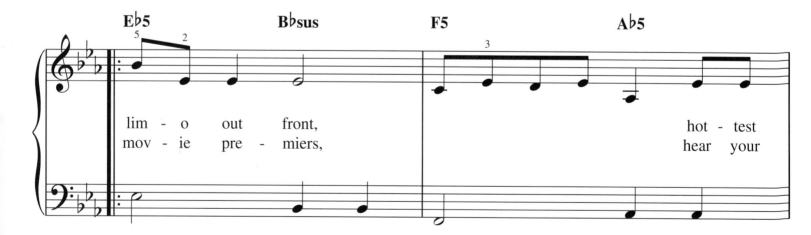

lim - o out front,
mov - ie pre - miers,

hot - test
hear your

styles, ev - 'ry shoe, ev - 'ry col - or. Yeah, when you're
songs on the ra - di - o. Liv - ing

fa - mous, it can be kind of fun. It's real - ly
two lives is a lit - tle weird, but

you, but no one ev - er dis - cov - ers.
school's cool, 'cause no - bod - y knows.

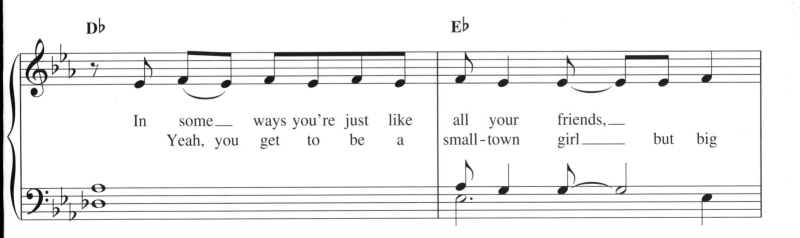

In some ways you're just like all your friends,
Yeah, you get to be a small - town girl but big

4

but on - stage you're a star.
time when you play your gui - tar.

You get the

best of both worlds. Chill it out, take it slow,— then you

rock out the show.— You get the best of both— worlds.

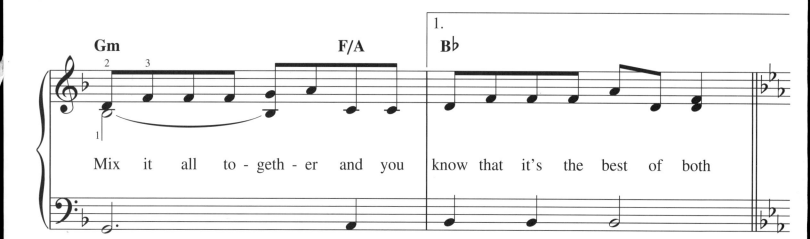

Mix it all to - geth - er and you know that it's the best of both

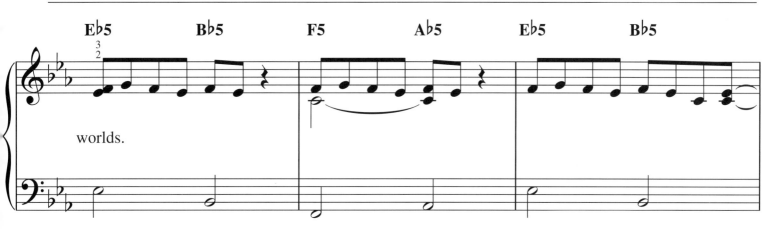

worlds.

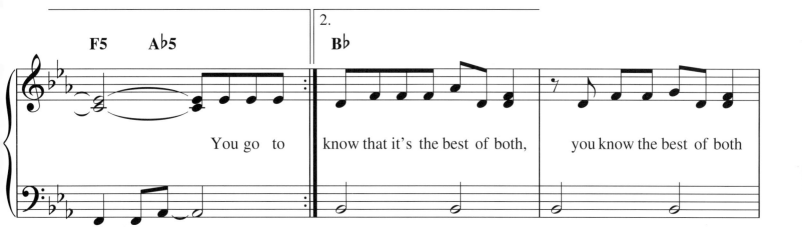

2.

You go to | know that it's the best of both, | you know the best of both

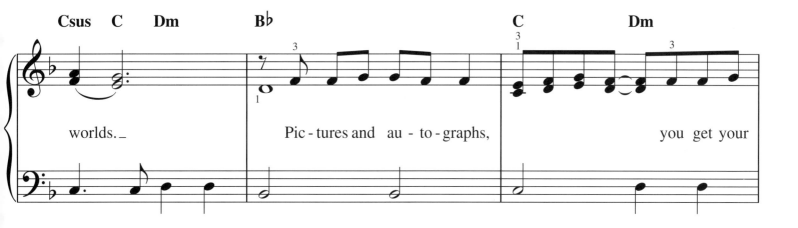

worlds. _ | Pic - tures and au - to - graphs, | you get your

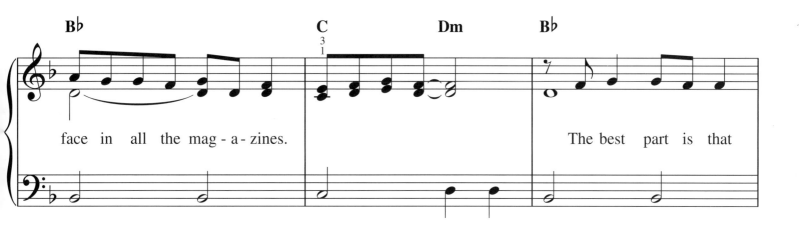

face in all the mag - a - zines. | | The best part is that

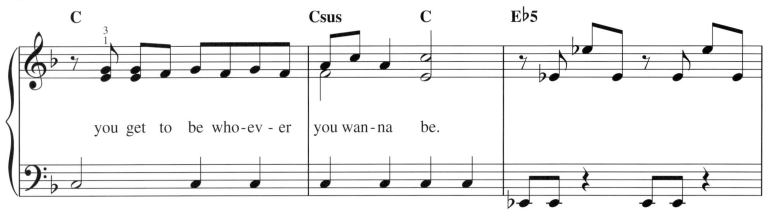

you get to be who-ev - er you wan-na be.

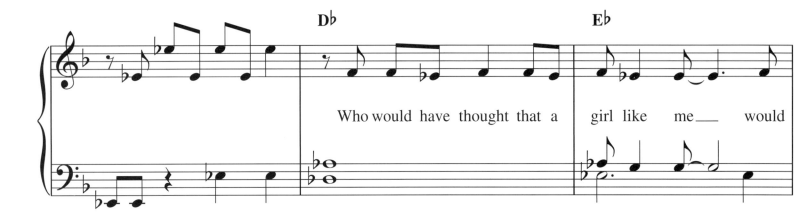

Who would have thought that a girl like me____ would

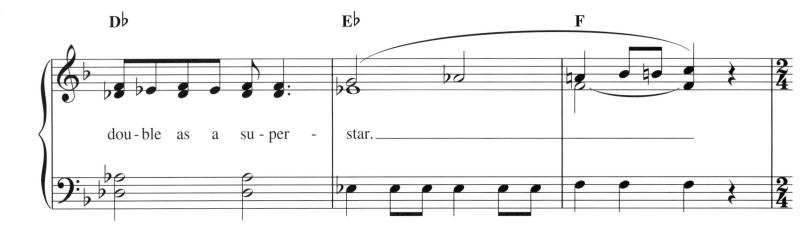

dou-ble as a su-per - star.____

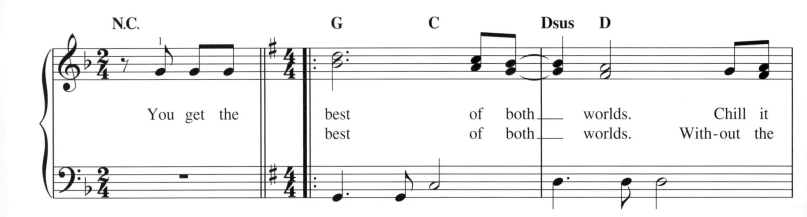

You get the / best of both____ worlds. Chill it
best of both____ worlds. With-out the

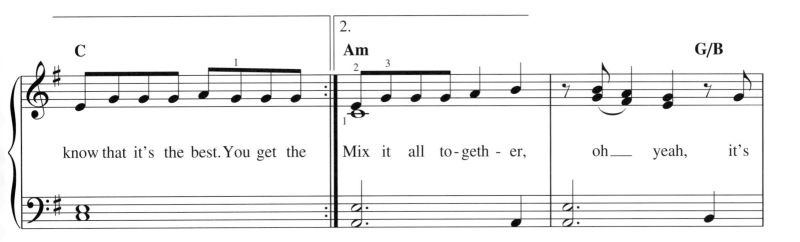

WHO SAID

Words and Music by MATTHEW GERRARD,
ROBBIE NEVIL and JAY LANDERS

I'm more than just

your av - 'rage girl.   I like to turn me up

and show the world.

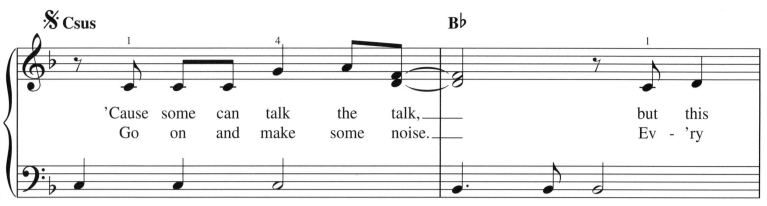

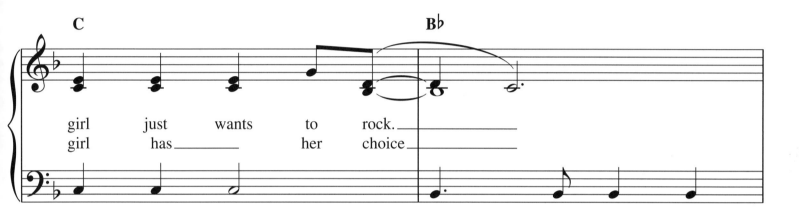

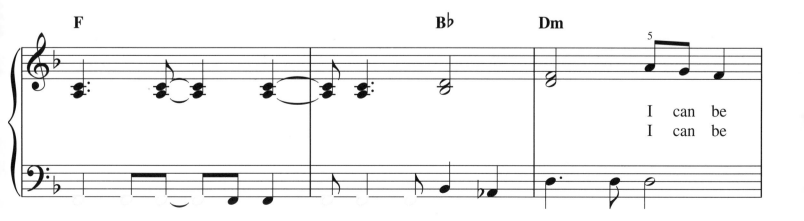

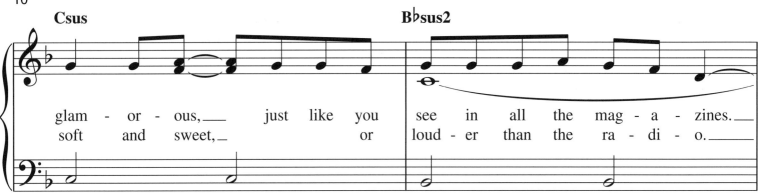

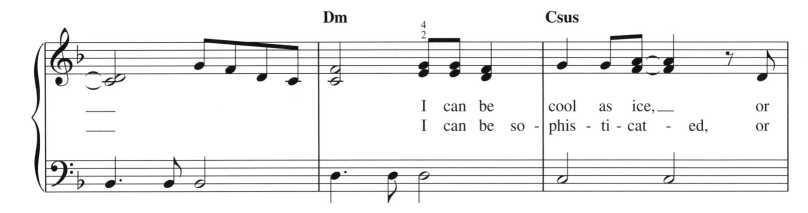

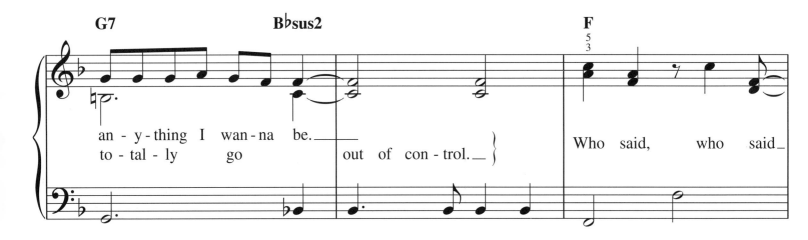

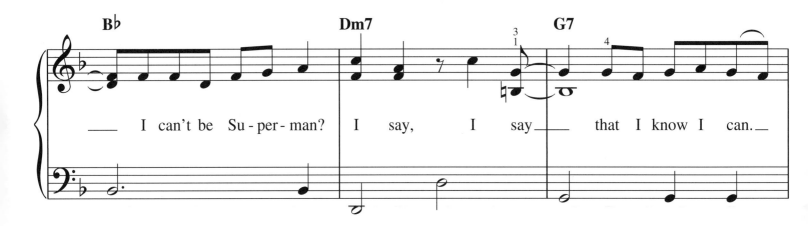

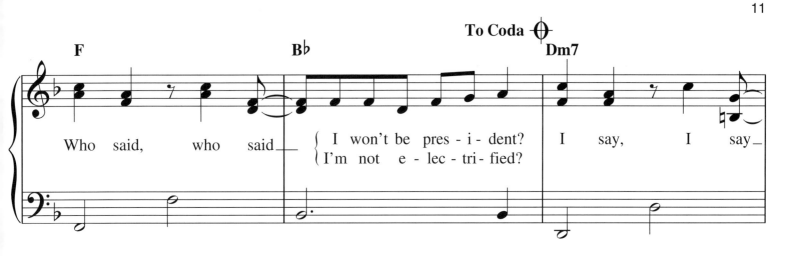

To Coda ⊕

Who said, who said
{ I won't be pres - i - dent?
{ I'm not e - lec - tri - fied?
I say, I say___

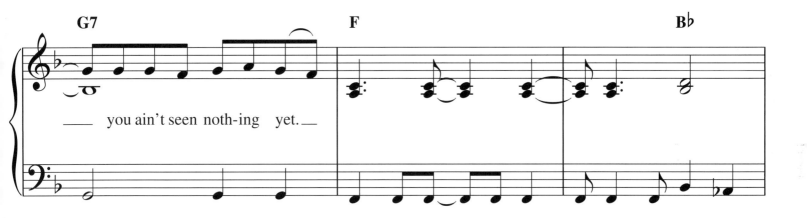

___ you ain't seen noth-ing yet.___

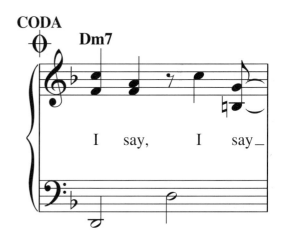

D.S. al Coda

CODA ⊕

I say, I say___

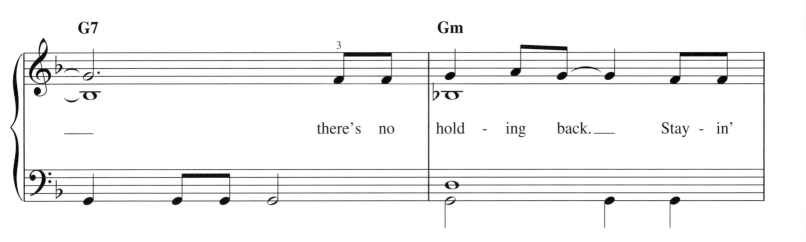

___ there's no hold - ing back.___ Stay - in'

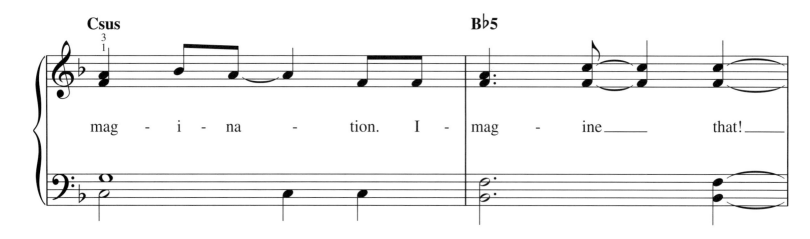

I say, I say___ that I know I can.___ Who said, who said___

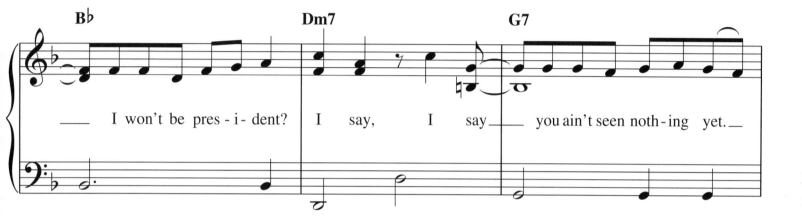

___ I won't be pres - i - dent? I say, I say___ you ain't seen noth-ing yet.___

You ain't seen noth-ing yet.___

JUST LIKE YOU

Words and Music by ANDREW DODD
and ADAM WATTS

Moderately fast

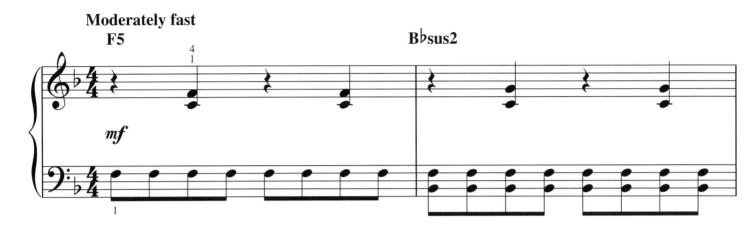

So what you see is only half the story; there's another side____ of me.

be treated differently.____ I wanna keep it all____ in-

side.

I'm the girl you know, but I'm

Half the time I've got____ my

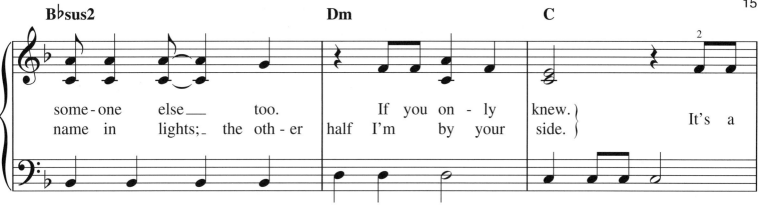

some-one else___ too.
name in lights;___ the oth-er half I'm by your

If you on-ly knew.} side.} It's a

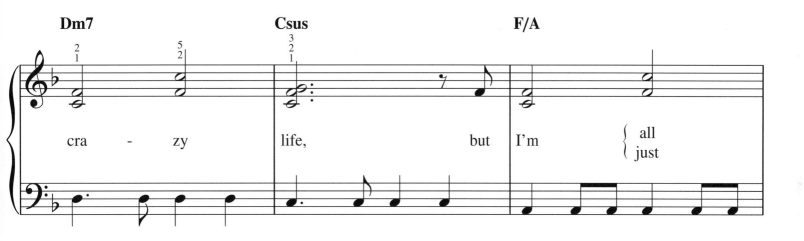

cra - zy life, but I'm {all
{just

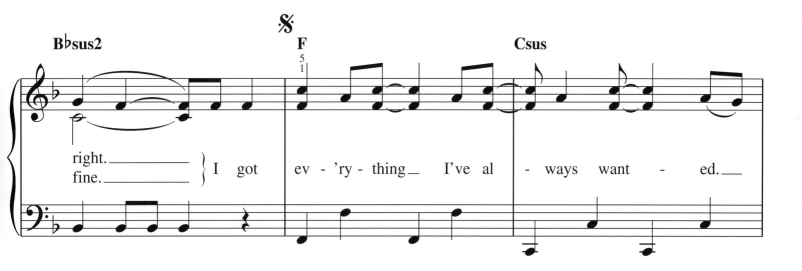

right._____ {I got ev-'ry-thing___ I've al - ways want - ed.___
fine._____

I'm liv-ing the dream.___ So yeah, ev-'ry-thing___ I've al -

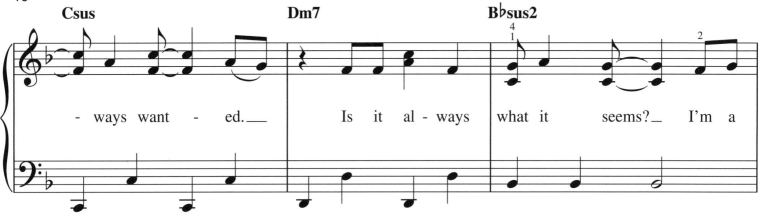

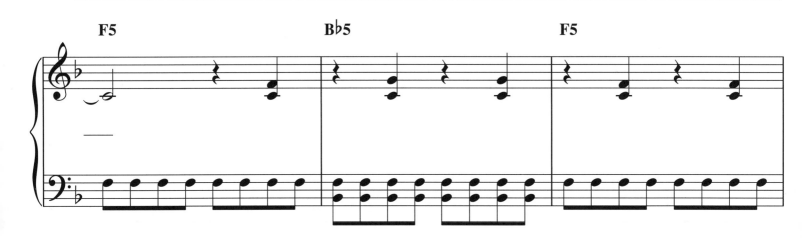

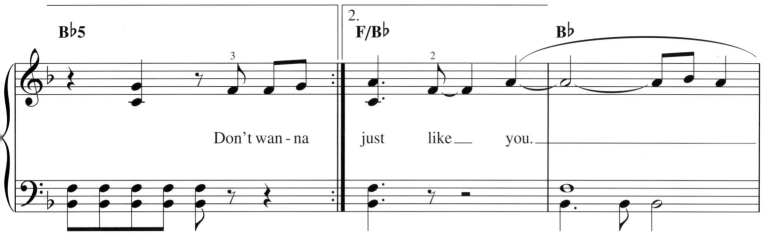

Don't wan - na just like___ you.___

___ Yeah, y - y - yeah. Can't you

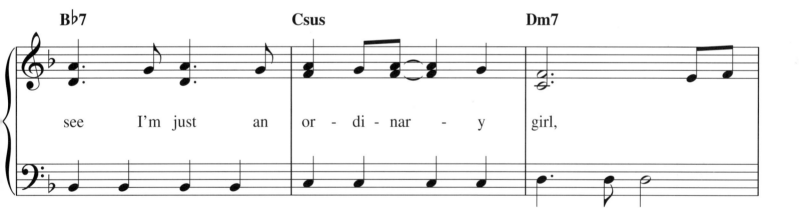

see I'm just an or - di - nar - y girl,

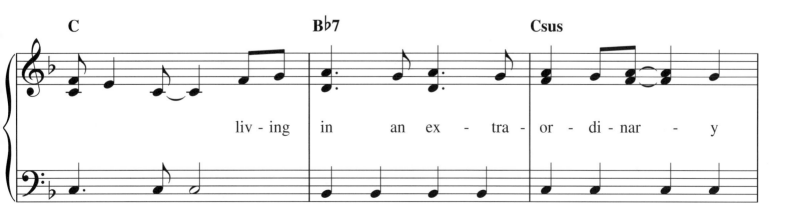

liv - ing in an ex - tra - or - di - nar - y

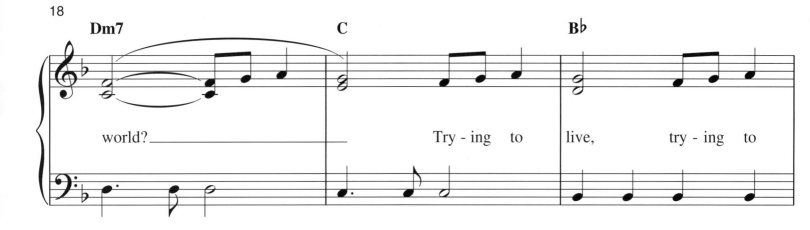

Dm7   **C**   **B♭**

world?_____   Try-ing to live,   try-ing to

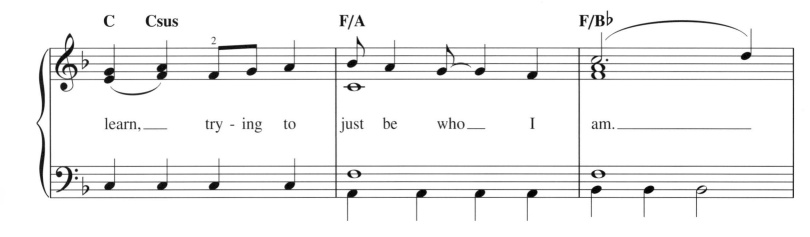

C   **Csus**   **F/A**   **F/B♭**

learn,___ try-ing to   just be who___ I   am._____

F5   **B♭5**   **F5**

Who I am.

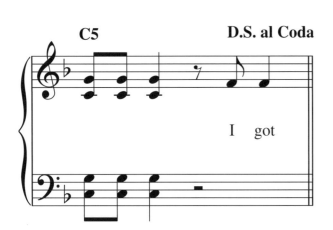

C5   **D.S. al Coda**

I got

CODA   **B♭sus2**

just like___ you.___

PUMPIN' UP THE PARTY

Words and Music by
JAMIE HOUSTON

Moderately fast

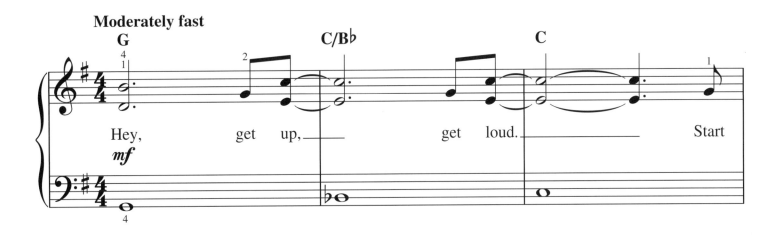

Hey, get up, get loud. Start

pump-in' up the par-ty now.

It's the

same old, same grind, but we don't feel we're wast-ing time.
They can't, we can. Par-ents might not un-der-stand

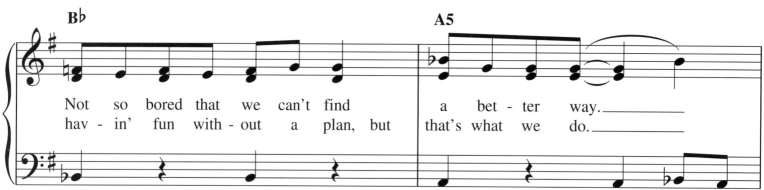

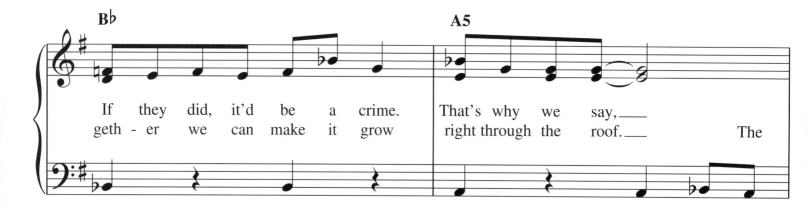

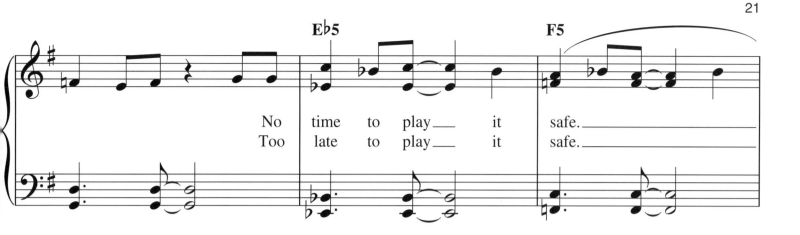

No time to play___ it safe.___
Too late to play___ it safe.___

Hey, get up,___ get loud.___

___ Start pump-in' up the par-ty now. Hey, get up,___

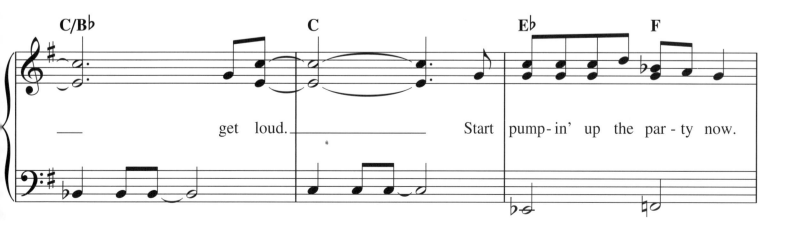

___ get loud.___ Start pump-in' up the par-ty now.

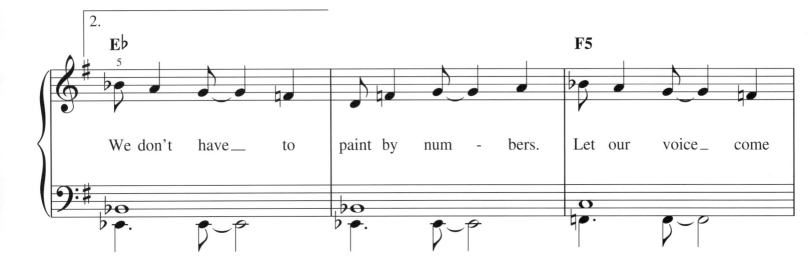

We don't have___ to paint by num - bers. Let our voice___ come

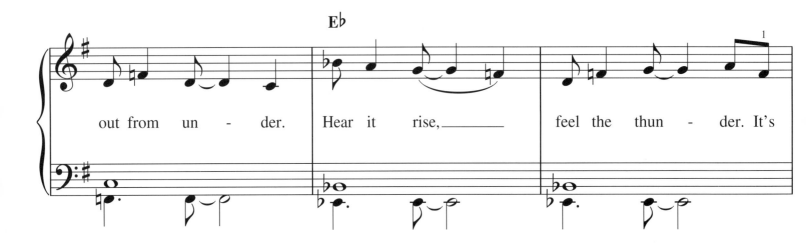

out from un - der. Hear it rise,_____ feel the thun - der. It's

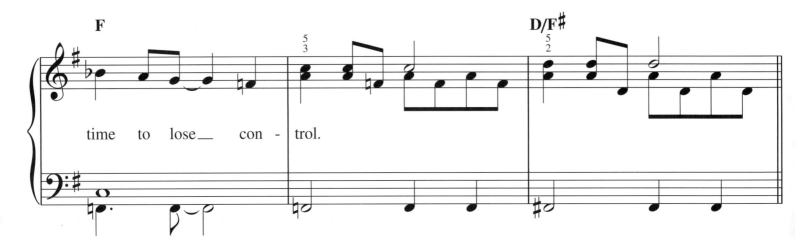

time to lose___ con - trol.

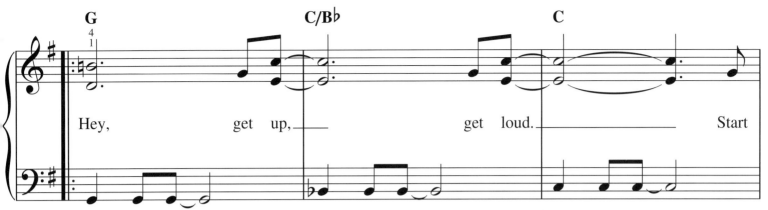

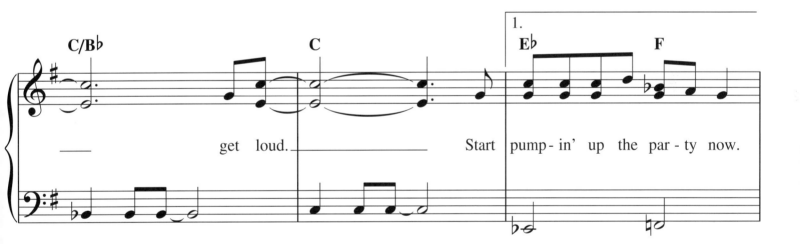

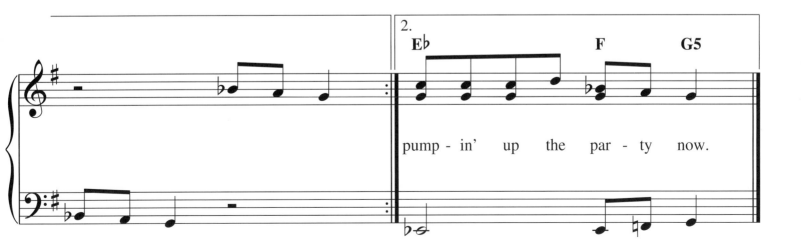

IF WE WERE A MOVIE

Words and Music by JEANNIE LURIE
and HOLLY MATHIS

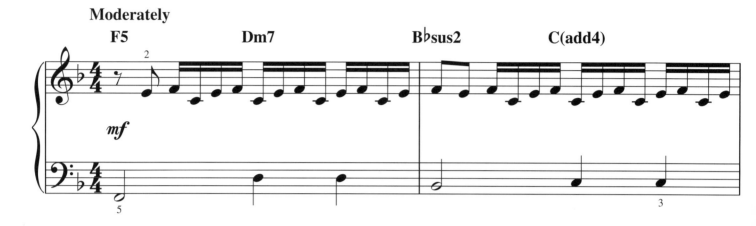

Uh - oh, there you go a - gain, talk - in' cin - e - mat - ic.
Yeah, yeah, when you call me___ I can hear it in your

Yeah, you, you're charm - ing, got ev - 'ry - bod - y star - struck.
voice. Oh, sure, you want to see me and tell me all a - bout her.

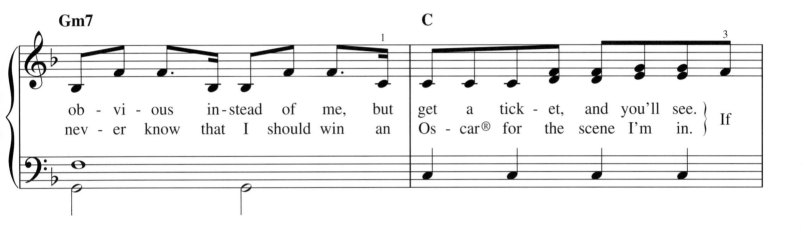

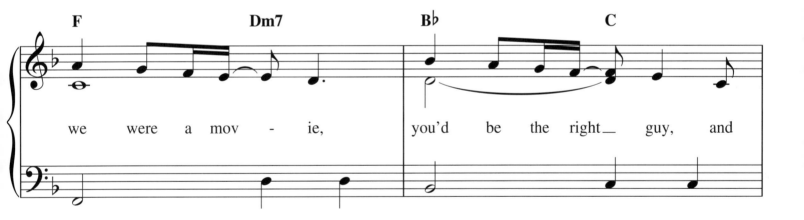

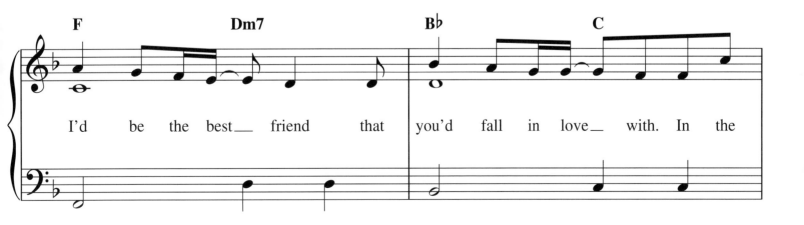

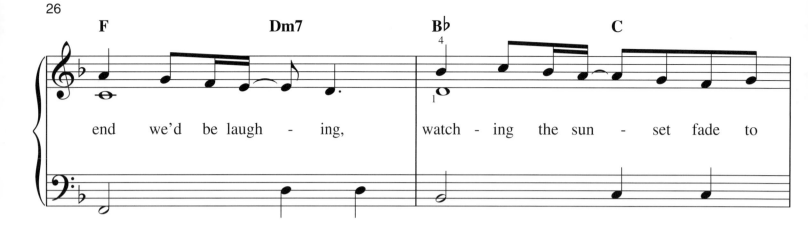

end we'd be laugh - ing, watch - ing the sun - set fade to

black, show the names, play the hap - py song.

Wish I could tell you there's a twist, some kind of he - ro in dis-

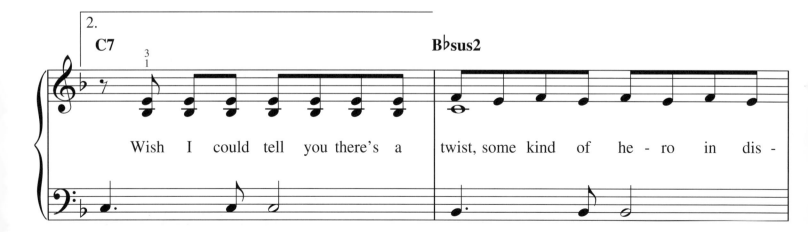

guise, and we're to - geth - er, it's for real,___ now play - ing.

Wish I could tell you there's a kiss, like some-thing more than in my

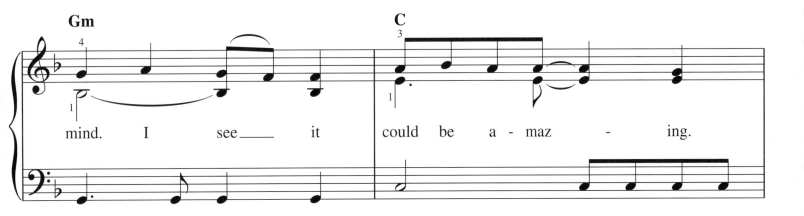

mind. I see___ it could be a - maz - ing.

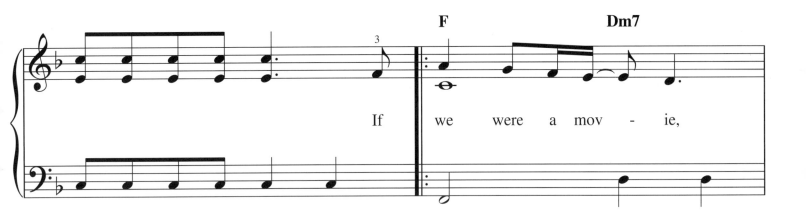

If we were a mov - ie,

B♭   **C**   **F**   **Dm7**

you'd be the right_ guy, and I'd be the best_ friend that

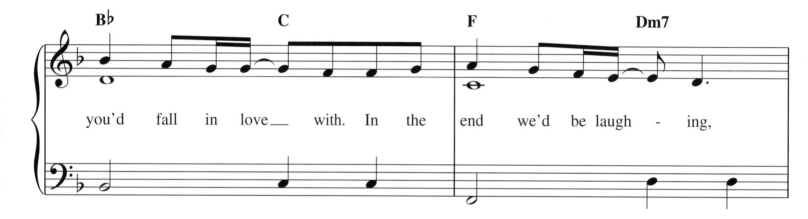

B♭   **C**   **F**   **Dm7**

you'd fall in love_ with. In the end we'd be laugh - ing,

B♭   **C**   **F**   **Dm7**

watch - ing the sun - set fade to black, show the names, play the

1.
B♭

hap - py song.   If

2.
B♭   **F**

hap - py song.

I GOT NERVE

Words and Music by JEANNIE LURIE,
KEN HAUPTMAN and ARUNA ABRAMS

We have-n't met, and that's o - kay, 'cause you will be ask-
E - lec - tri - fied, I'm on the wire, get - tin' to-geth-

-ing for me one day. Don't wan-na wait in line;
-er, and we're on fire. What I say, you heard:

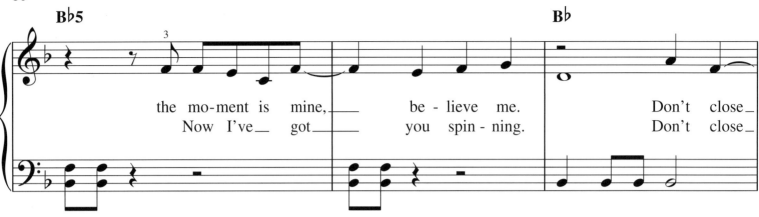

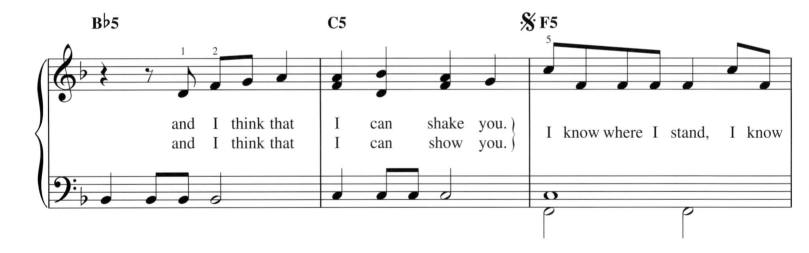

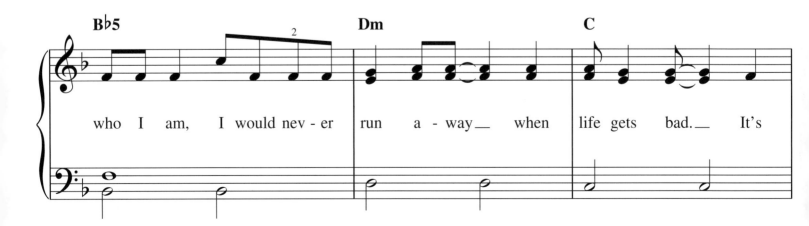

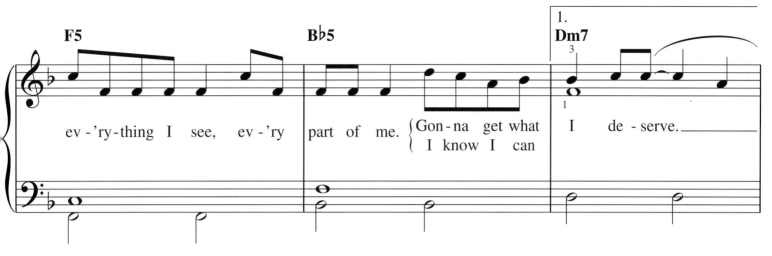

ev-'ry-thing I see, ev-'ry part of me. {Gon-na get what I de - serve.___
I know I can

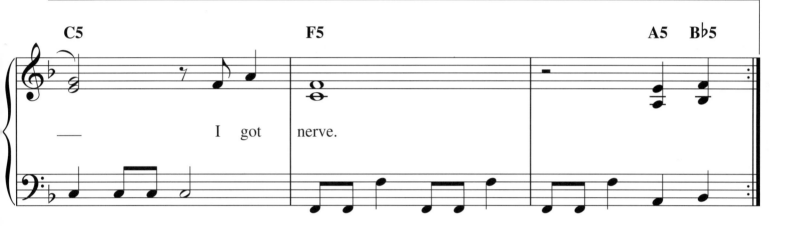

___ I got nerve.

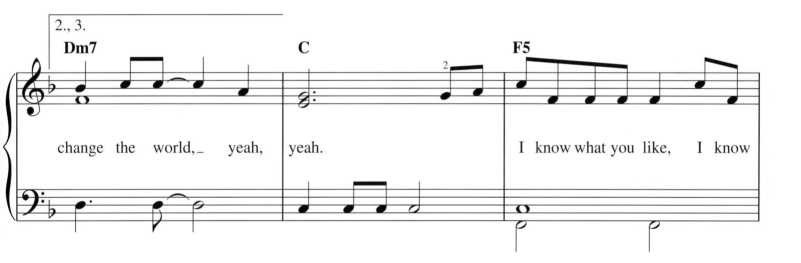

change the world,_ yeah, yeah. I know what you like, I know

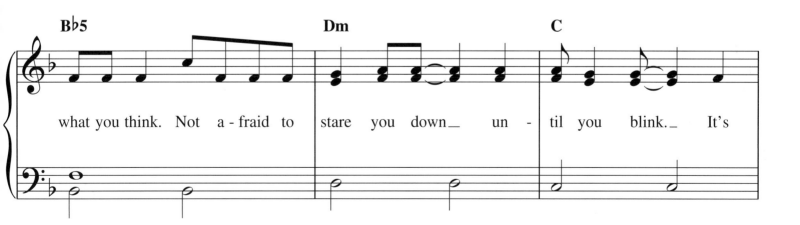

what you think. Not a-fraid to stare you down_ un - til you blink._ It's

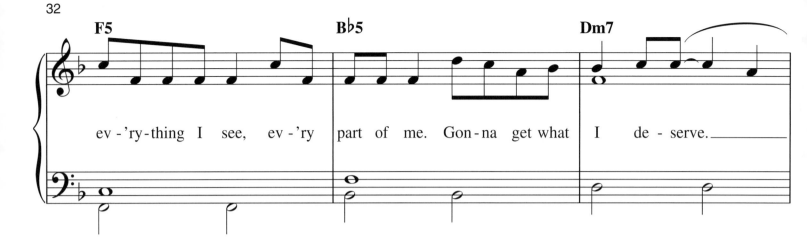

ev-'ry-thing I see, ev-'ry part of me. Gon-na get what I de - serve.

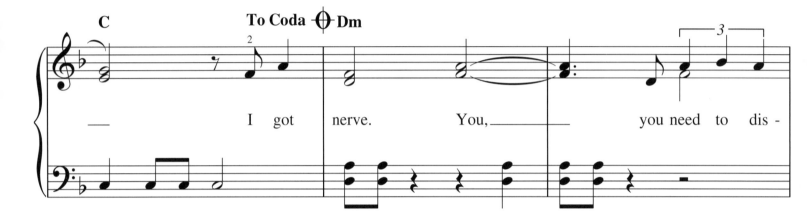

I got nerve. You,____ you need to dis-

cov - er____ who can

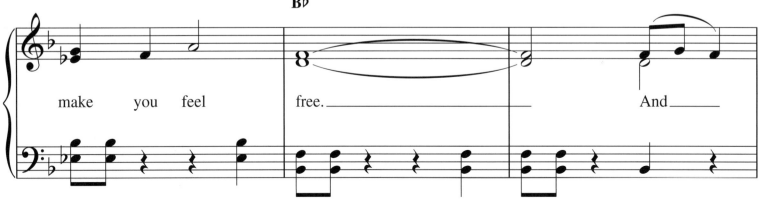

make you feel free.____ And____

I, _____ I need to un - cov - er _____

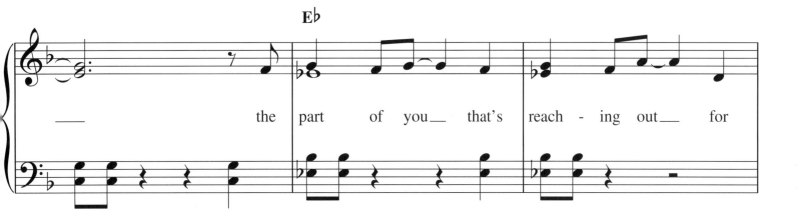

___ the part of you__ that's reach - ing out__ for

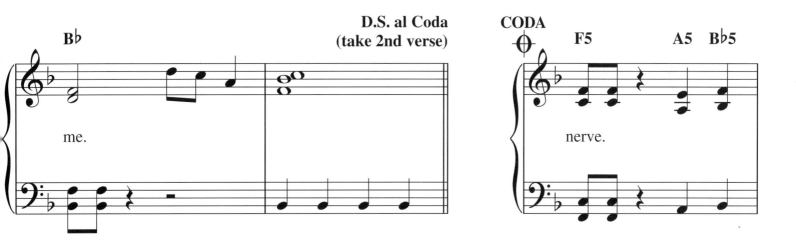

D.S. al Coda
(take 2nd verse)

me. nerve.

THE OTHER SIDE OF ME

Words and Music by MATTHEW GERRARD,
ROBBIE NEVIL and JAY LANDERS

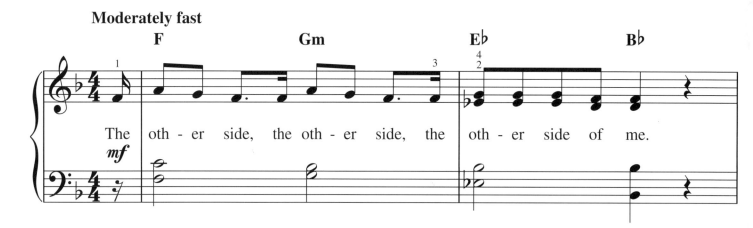

The oth-er side, the oth-er side, the oth-er side of me.

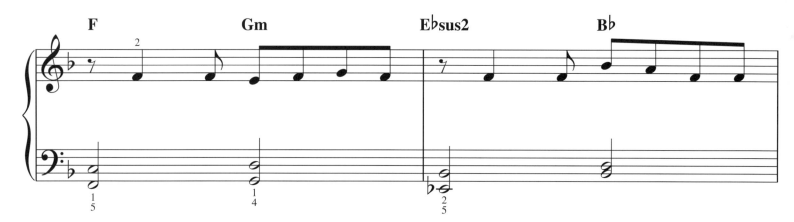

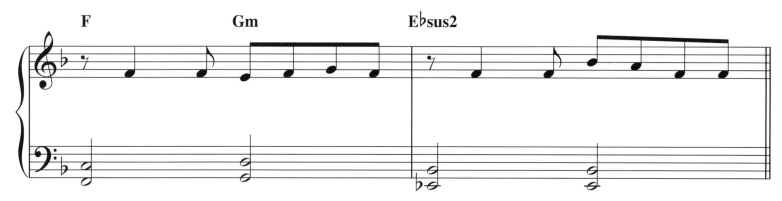

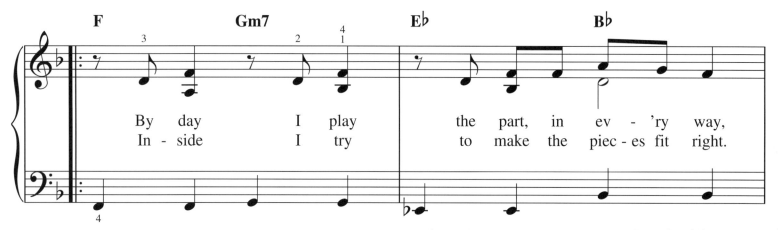

By day   I play   the part, in ev-'ry way,
In - side   I try   to make the piec-es fit right.

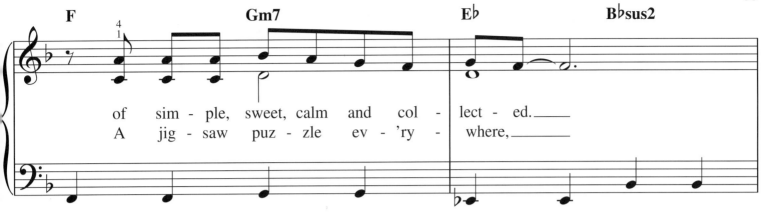

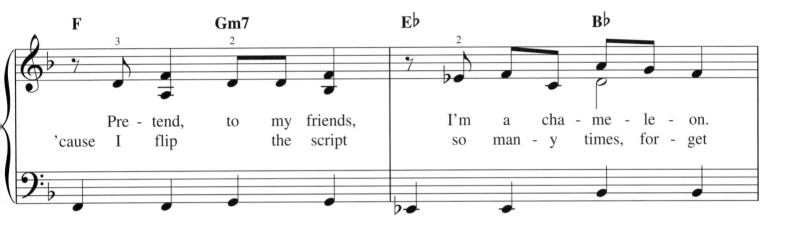

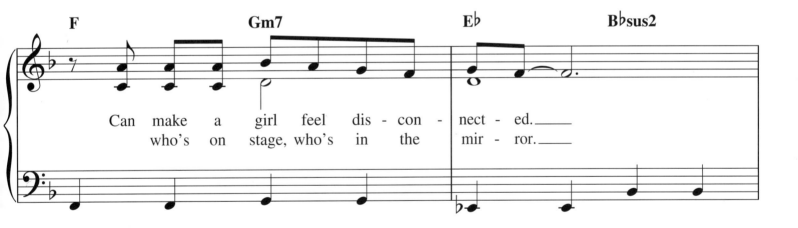

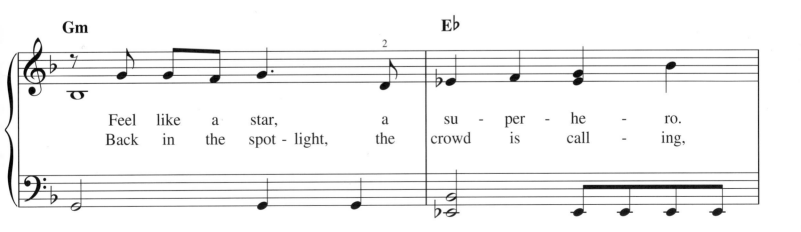

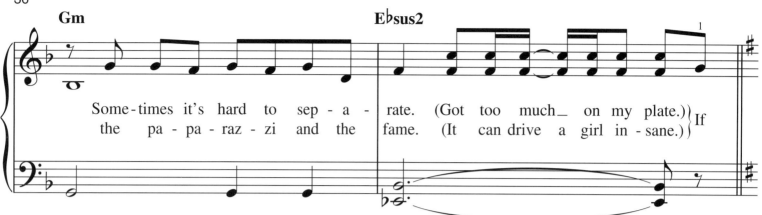

Some-times it's hard to sep-a-rate. (Got too much on my plate.)
the pa-pa-raz-zi and the fame. (It can drive a girl in-sane.) If

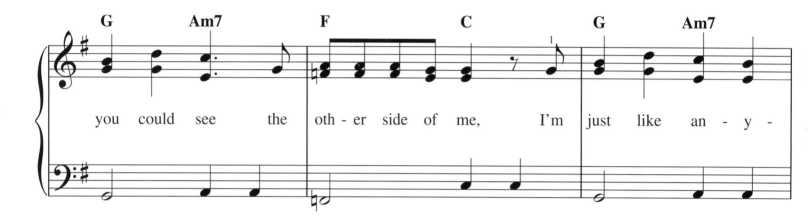

you could see the oth-er side of me, I'm just like an-y-

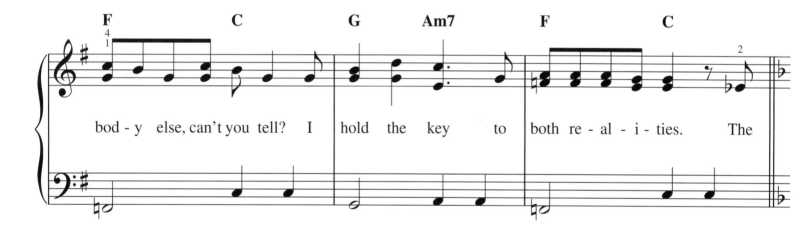

bod-y else, can't you tell? I hold the key to both re-al-i-ties. The

girl that I want you to know, if on-ly I could show the

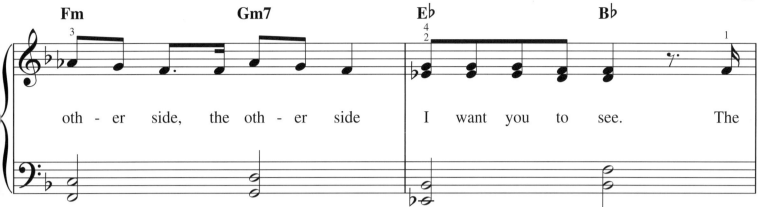

other side, the oth - er side I want you to see. The

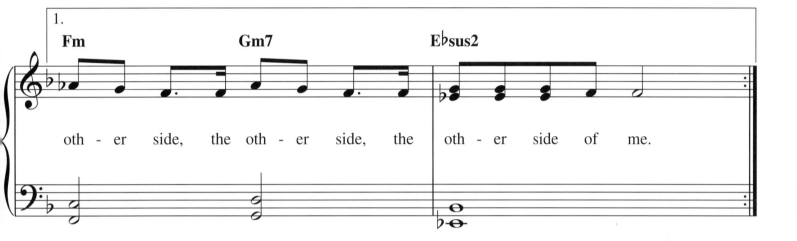

1.

other side, the oth - er side, the oth - er side of me.

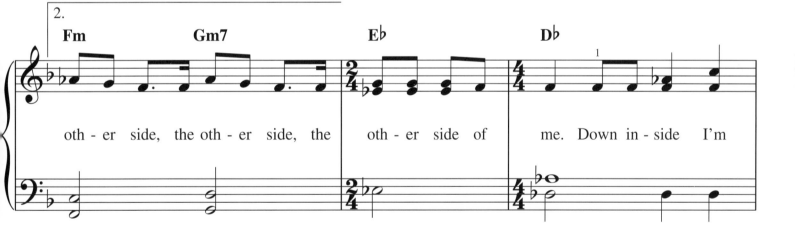

2.

other side, the oth - er side, the oth - er side of me. Down in - side I'm

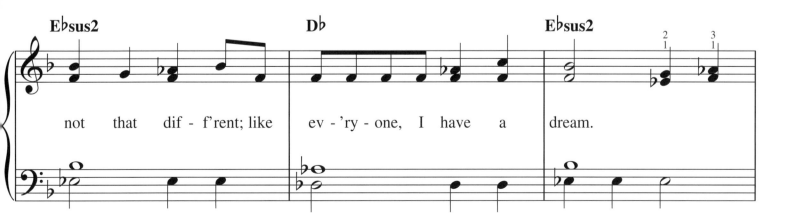

not that dif - f'rent; like ev - 'ry - one, I have a dream.

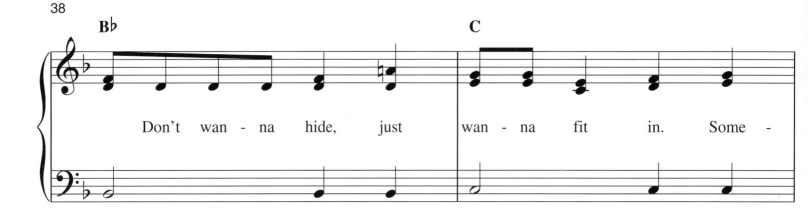

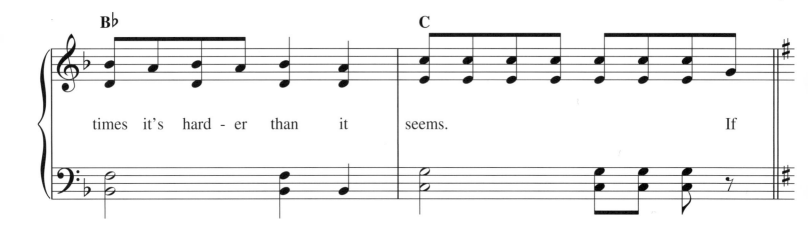

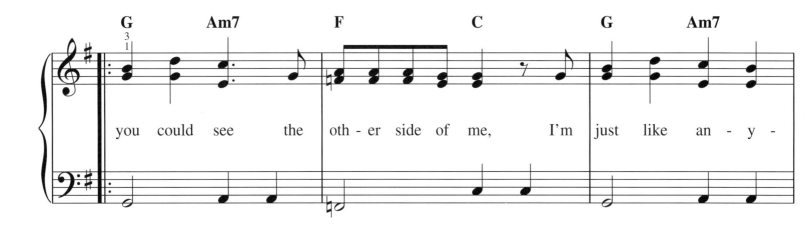

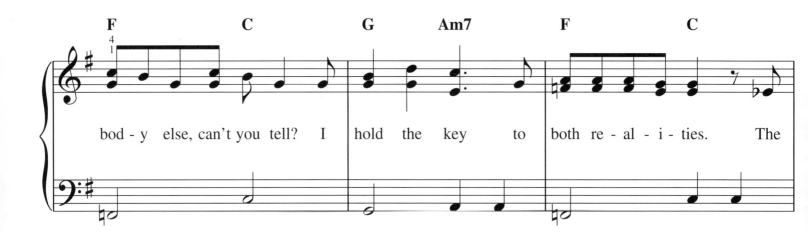

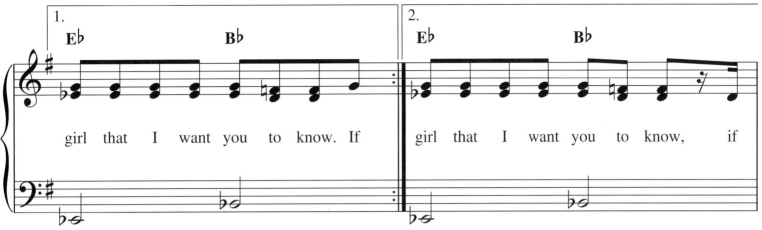

1.
Eb   Bb

girl that I want you to know. If

2.
Eb   Bb

girl that I want you to know, if

Eb   Bb   Gm   A5   F   C

on - ly I could show the oth - er side, the oth - er side I want you to see. The

Gm   A5   F   C   Gm   A5

oth - er side, the oth - er side, the oth - er side of me, the oth - er side, the oth - er side,

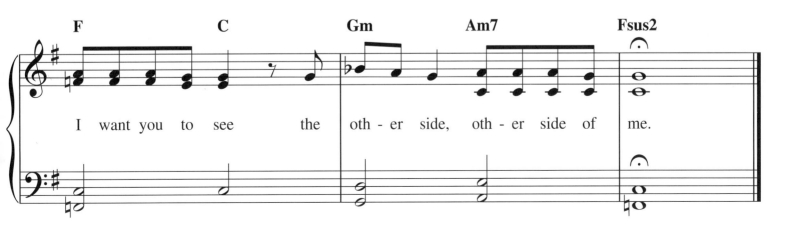

F   C   Gm   Am7   Fsus2

I want you to see the oth - er side, oth - er side of me.

THIS IS THE LIFE

Words and Music by JEANNIE LURIE
and SHARI SHORT

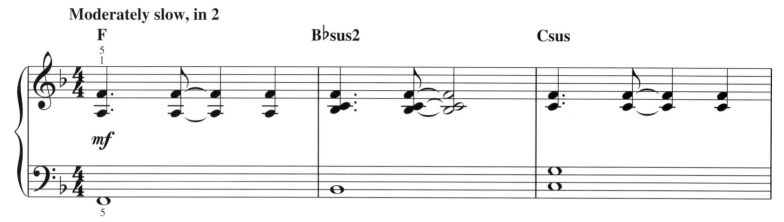

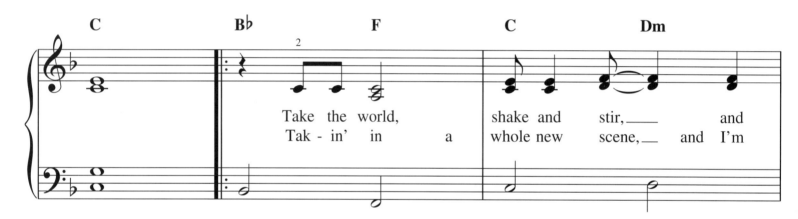

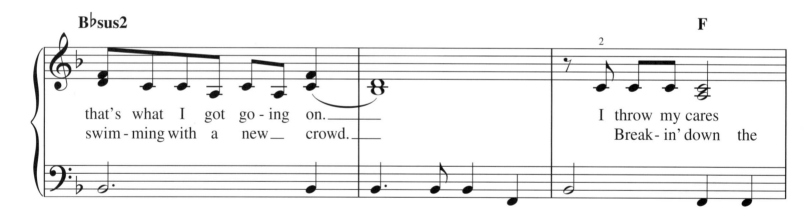

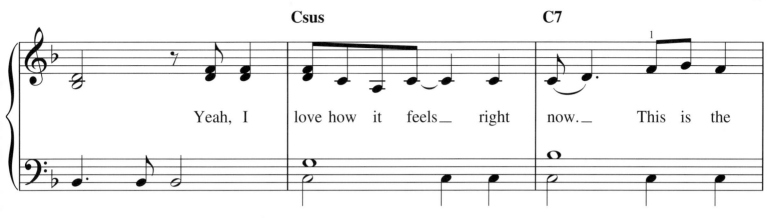

Csus C7

Yeah, I love how it feels__ right now.__ This is the

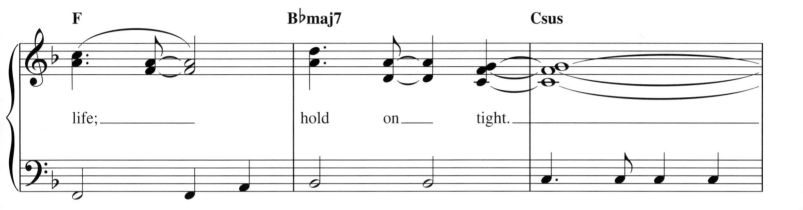

F B♭maj7 Csus

life;_____ hold on___ tight._____

F B♭maj7

___ And this is a dream._____ It's all I___ need._

Csus Gm7

___ You nev - er know where you'll find it,___ and

42

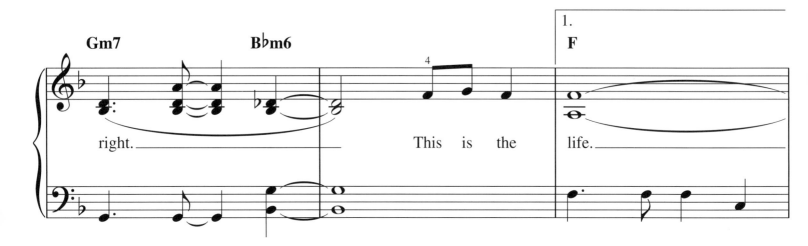

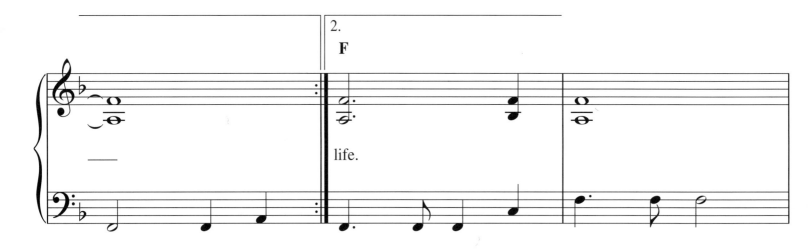

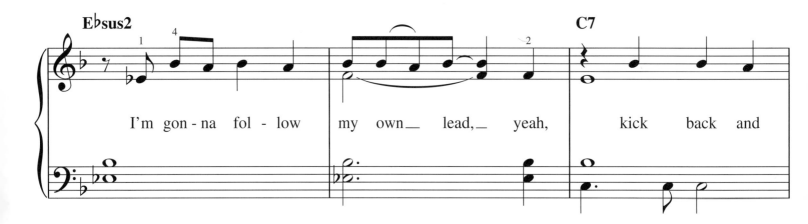

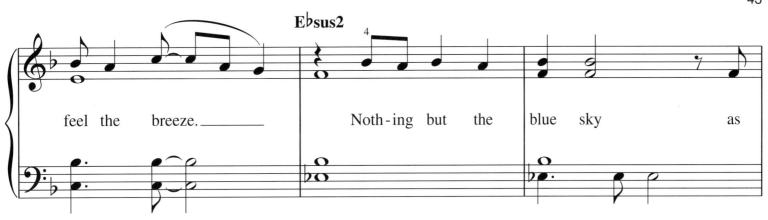

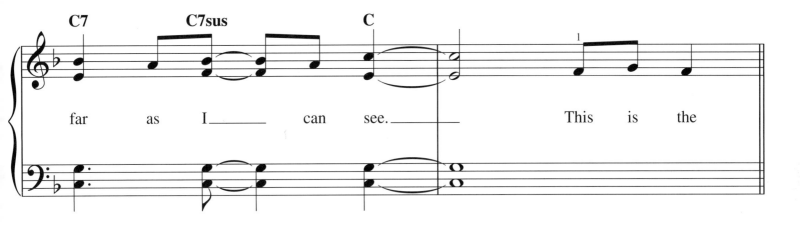

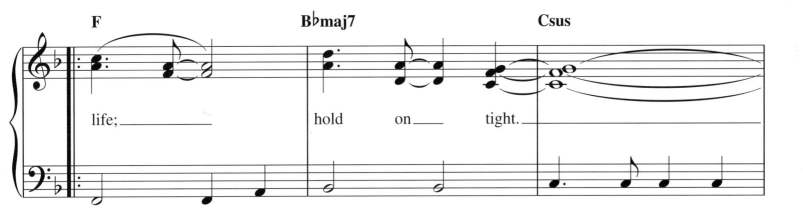

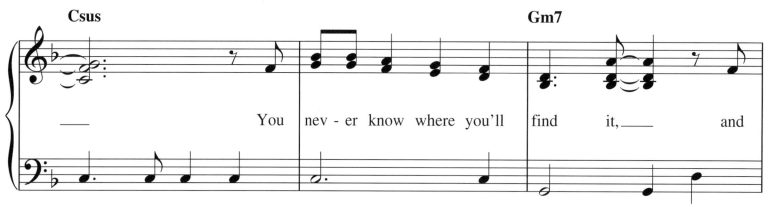

Csus   Gm7

_____ You nev-er know where you'll find it, _____ and

C7   Gm7   C7

I'm gon-na take my time, yeah. _____ I'm still get-ting it

1.
Gm7   B♭m6

right. _____ This is the

2.
Gm7   B♭m6

right. _____

4

         F

_____ This is the life.

SHE'S NO YOU

Words and Music by MATTHEW GERRARD,
JESSE McCARTNEY and ROBBIE NEVIL

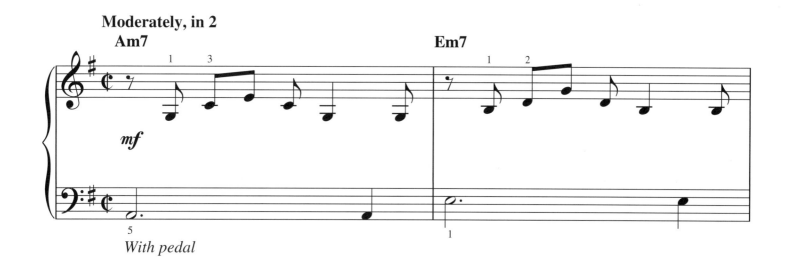

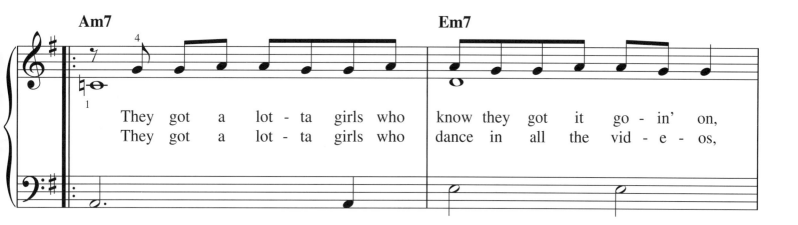

They got a lot-ta girls who know they got it go-in' on,
They got a lot-ta girls who dance in all the vid-e-os,

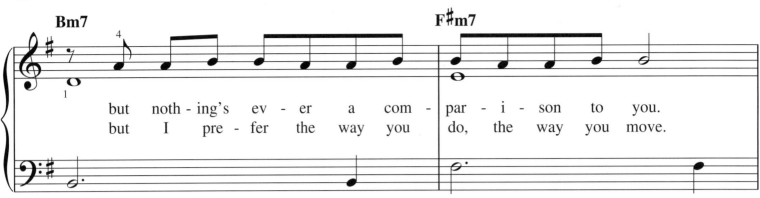

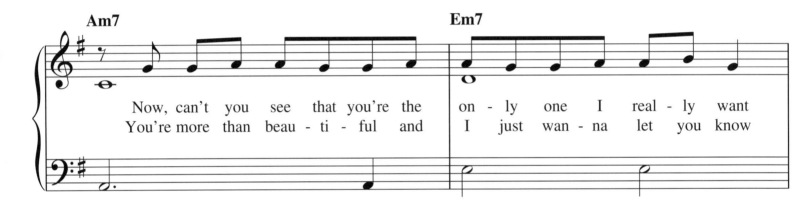

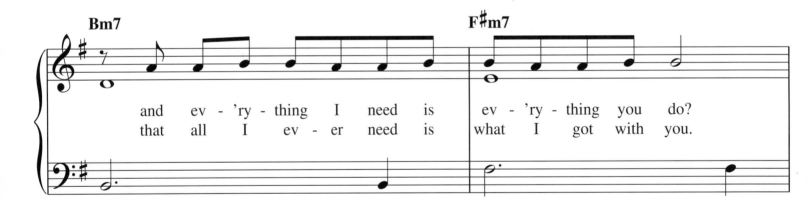

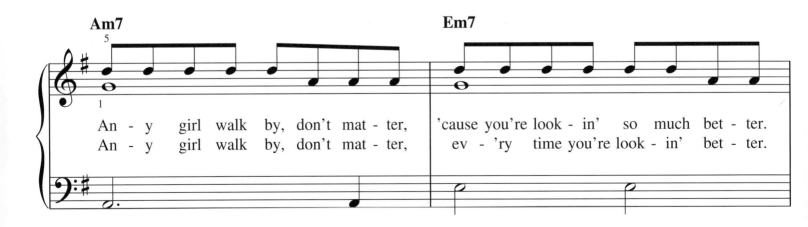

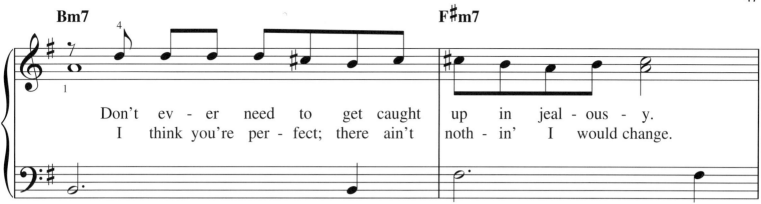

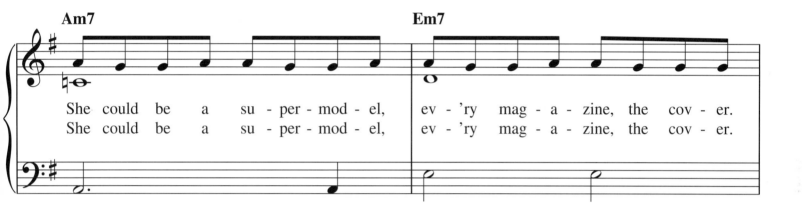

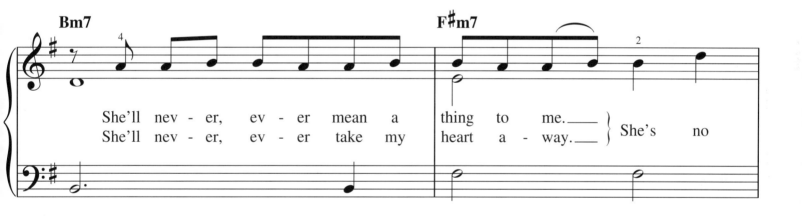

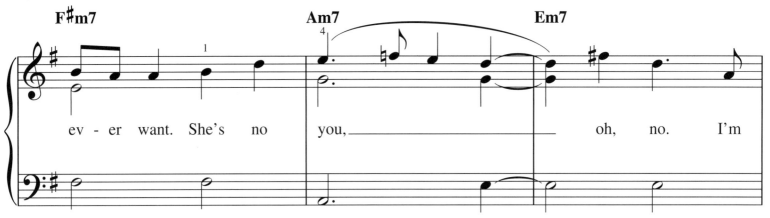

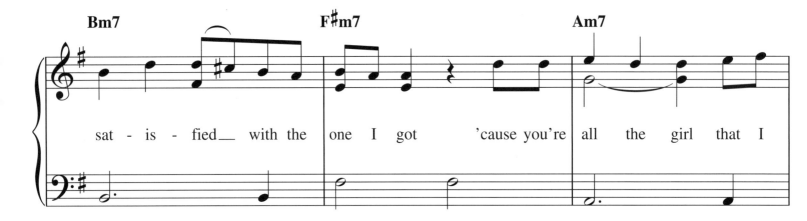

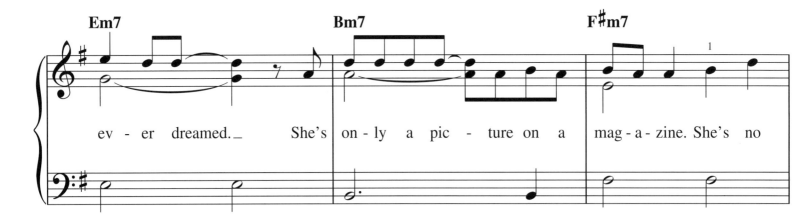

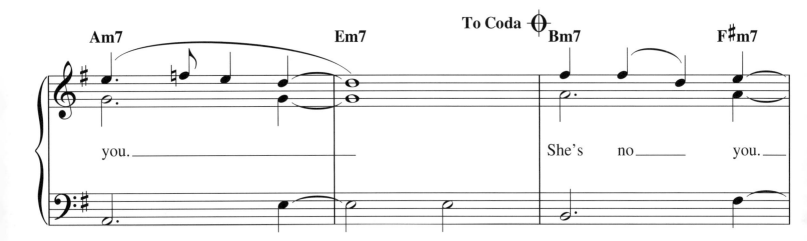

No one's ev - er gon - na get to me,__ oh,

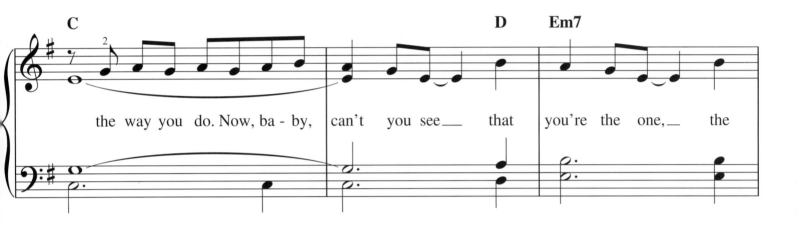

the way you do. Now, ba - by, can't you see__ that you're the one,__ the

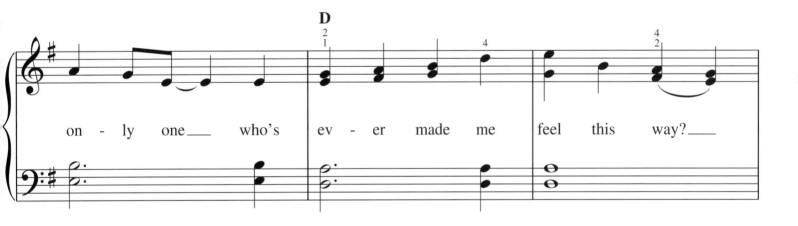

on - ly one__ who's ev - er made me feel this way?__

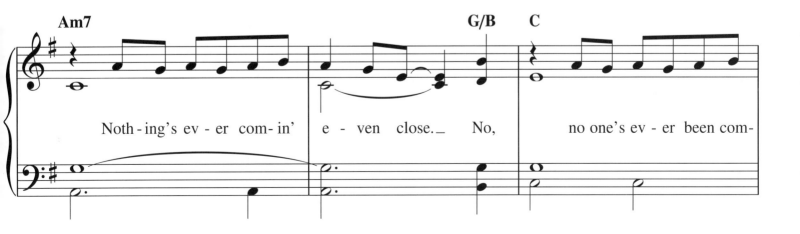

Noth - ing's ev - er com - in' e - ven close.__ No, no one's ev - er been com-

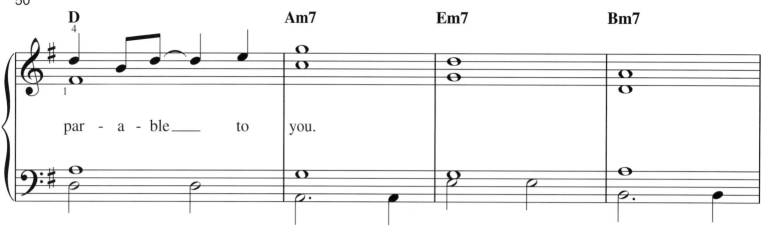

D **Am7** **Em7** **Bm7**

par - a - ble___ to you.

F#m7 **Am7** **Em7**

I don't want noth - in' I don't got.
You're all that, all that and then some.

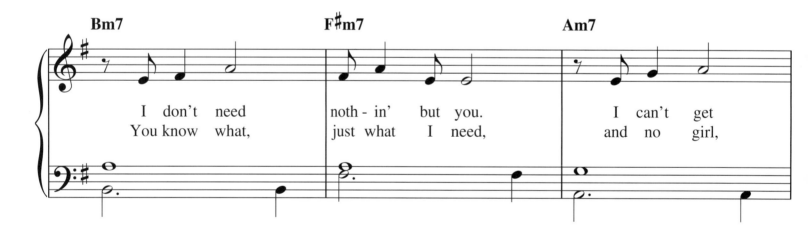

Bm7 **F#m7** **Am7**

I don't need noth - in' but you. I can't get
You know what, just what I need, and no girl,

Em7 1. **Bm7** **F#m7**

more than you give me, so don't stop an - y - thing you do.
no place,___ no - where

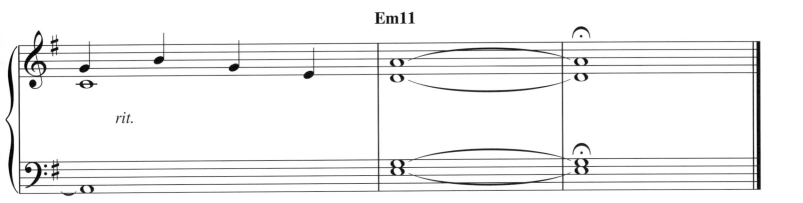

POP PRINCESS

Words and Music by
BEN ROMANS

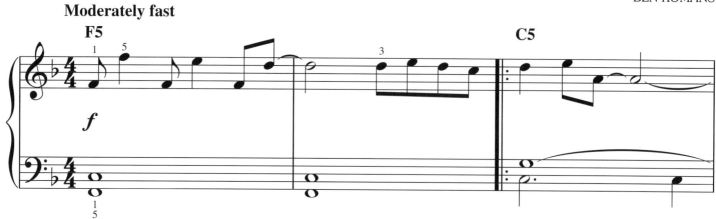

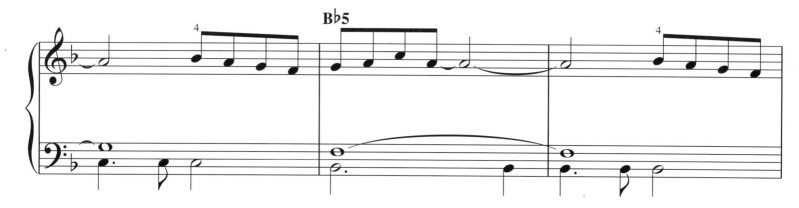

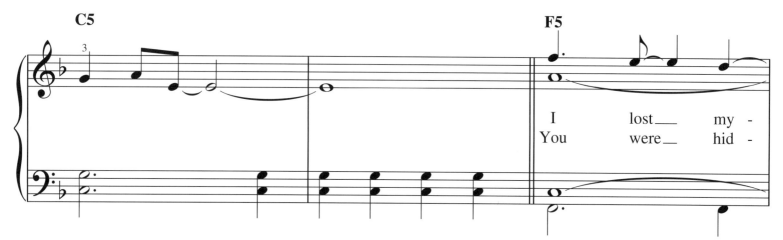

I lost___ my -
You were___ hid -

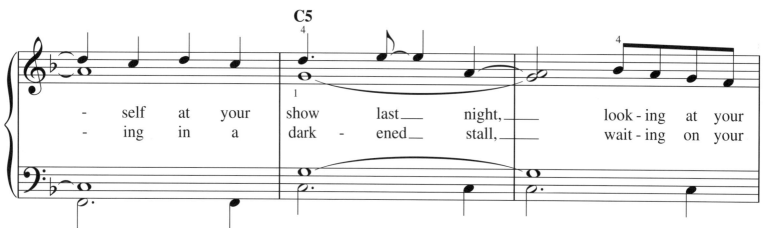

- self at your show last___ night,___ look - ing at your
- ing in a dark - ened___ stall,___ wait - ing on your

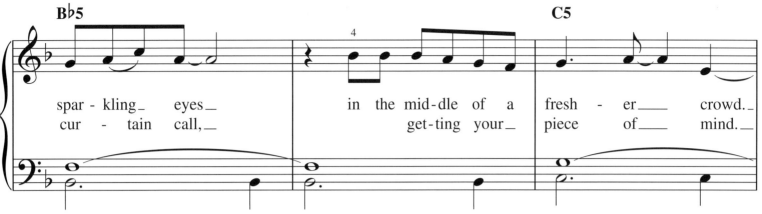

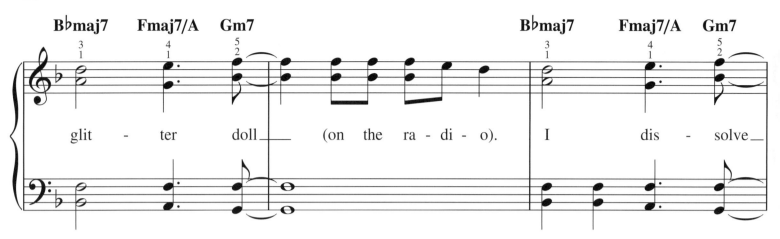

glit - ter doll___ (on the ra - di - o). I dis - solve___

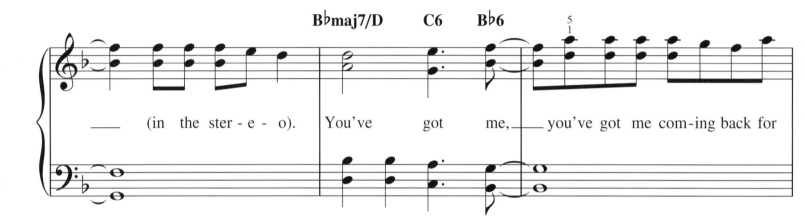

___ (in the ster - e - o). You've got me,___ you've got me com-ing back for

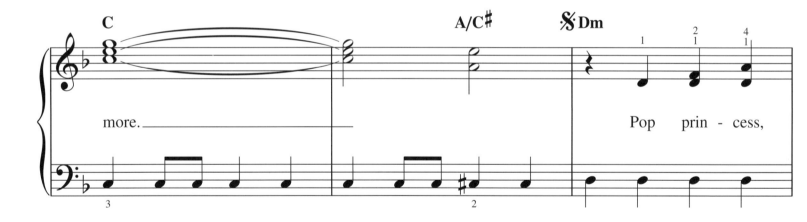

more.___ Pop prin - cess,

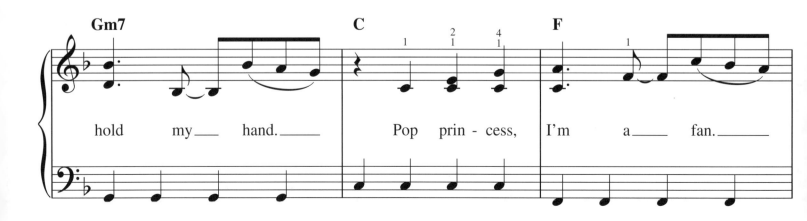

hold my___ hand.___ Pop prin - cess, I'm a___ fan.___

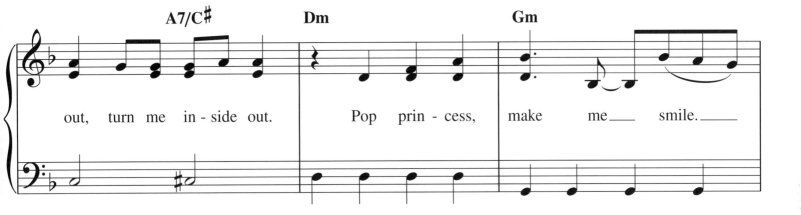

1. **F**

loud.

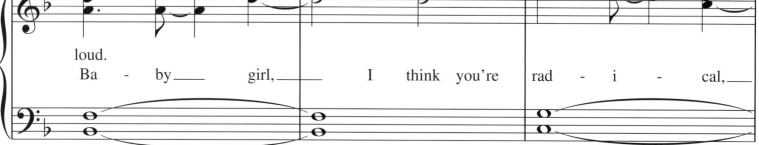

2. **B♭maj7**　　　　　　　　　　　**C**

loud.
Ba - by___ girl,___ I think you're rad - i - cal,___

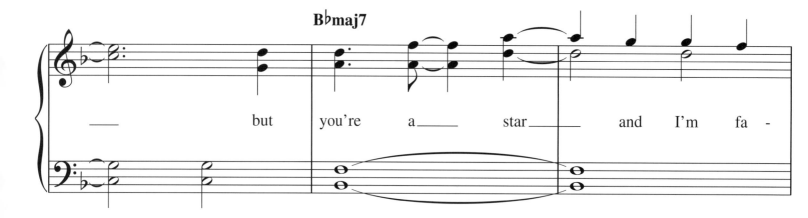

B♭maj7

___ but you're a___ star___ and I'm fa -

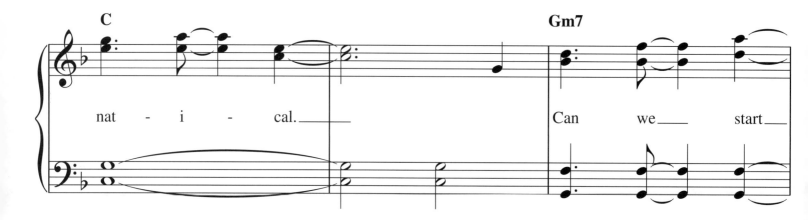

C　　　　　　　　　　**Gm7**

nat - i - cal.___ Can we___ start___

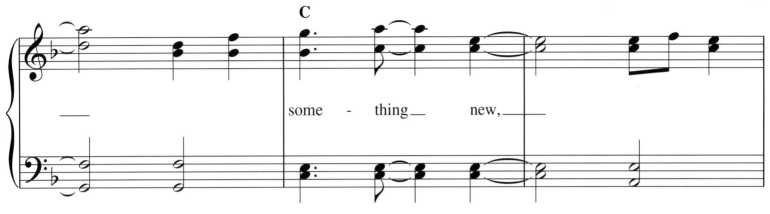

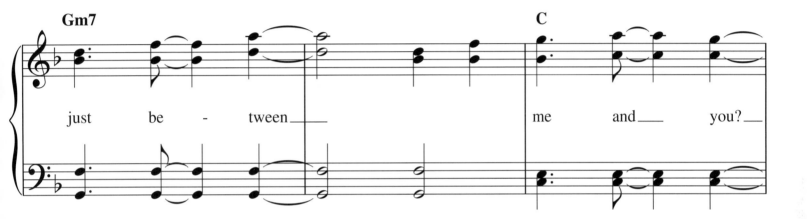

some - thing___ new,___ just be - tween___ me and___ you?___

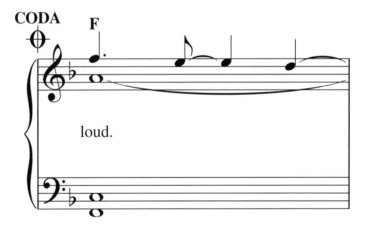

loud.

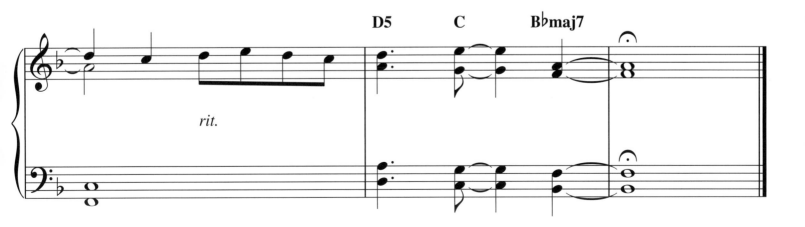

rit.

FIND YOURSELF IN YOU

Words and Music by MATTHEW GERRARD,
AMBER HEZLEP, JULIA ROSS and SARAH ROSS

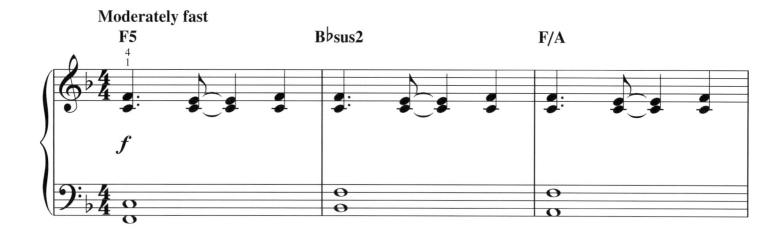

She's nev - er thought ___ that she would

get her sec - ond chance, run - ning so far ___

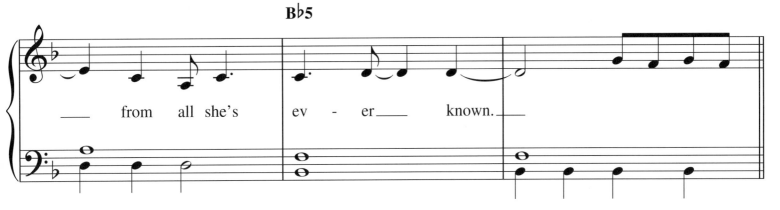

from all she's ev - er___ known.___

Con - vinced she lost___ all mean - ing, where did her___
Some - times peo - ple tell you. "Be like me___

___ dreams go? Still, she knew___ that there was
___ to fit in." Do you know___ your i - den - ti - ty's

some - thing___ more.___ Don't be
not in___ them?___

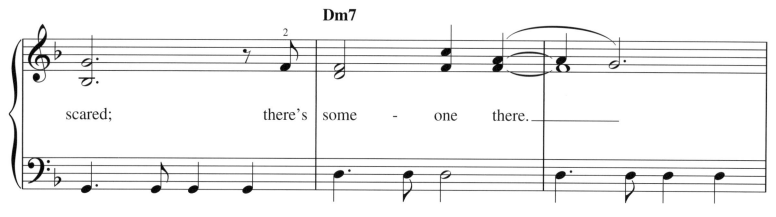

scared; there's some - one there._____

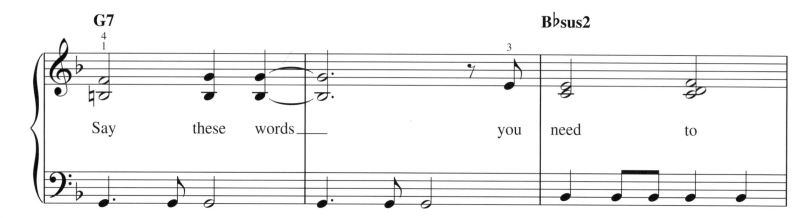

Say these words_____ you need to

hear:_____ Don't let an - y - bod - y tell you who_____ you

are._____ It's o - kay to let go;

you're that shoot - ing star._____ Re -

mem - ber all___ you wished for._____ Be - lieve it will___ be

true. You will nev - er find your - self an - y - where

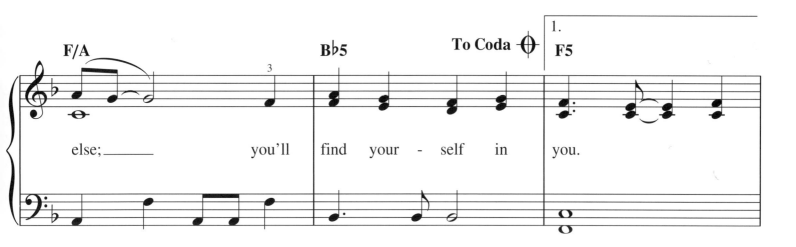

else;_____ you'll find your - self in you.

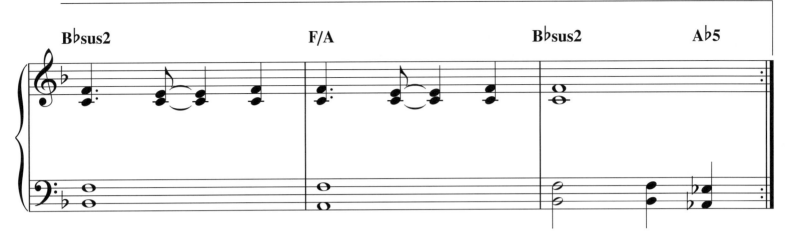

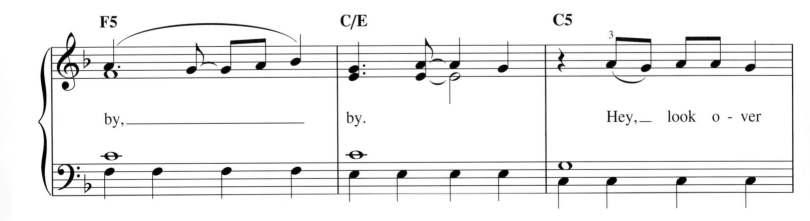

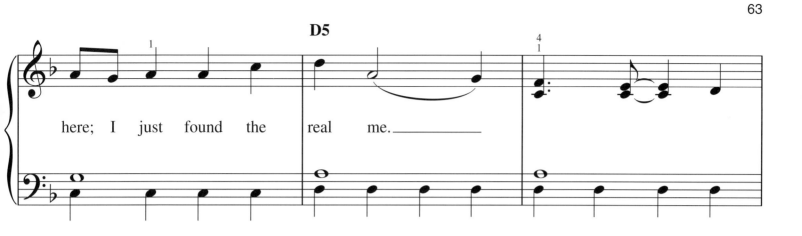

D5

here; I just found the real me._____

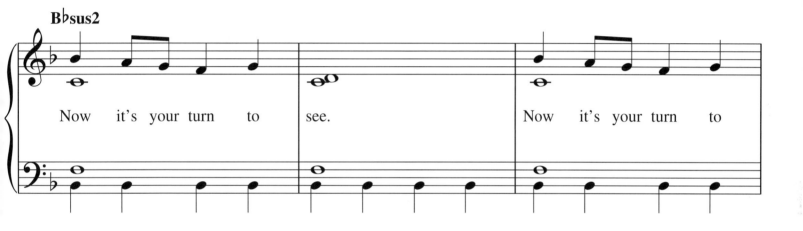

B♭sus2

Now it's your turn to see. Now it's your turn to

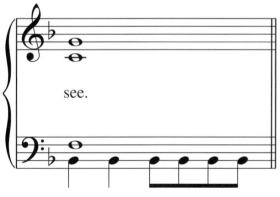

D.S. al Coda

see.

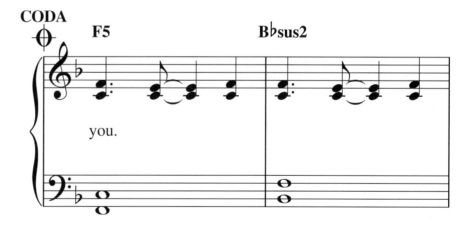

CODA
F5　　　　　　　**B♭sus2**

you.

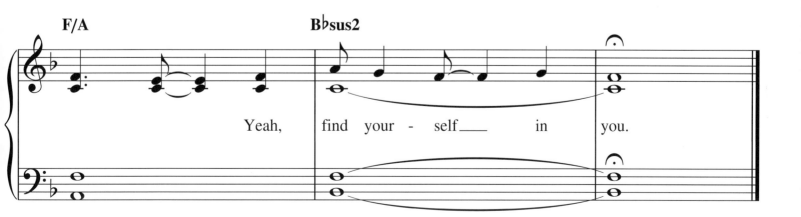

F/A　　　　　　　**B♭sus2**

Yeah, find your - self___ in you.

I LEARNED FROM YOU

Words and Music by MATTHEW GERRARD
and STEVE DIAMOND

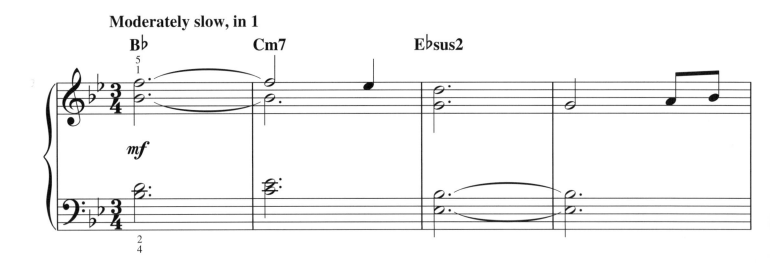

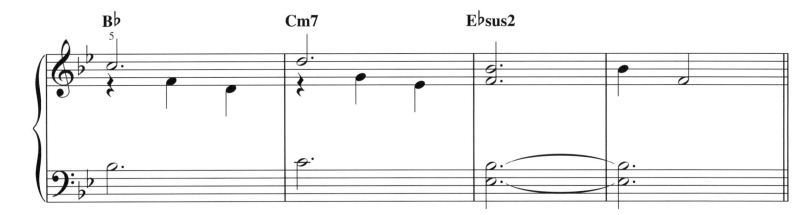

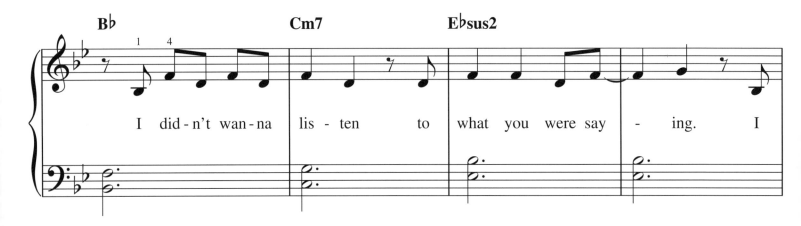

I did-n't wan-na lis-ten to what you were say - ing. I

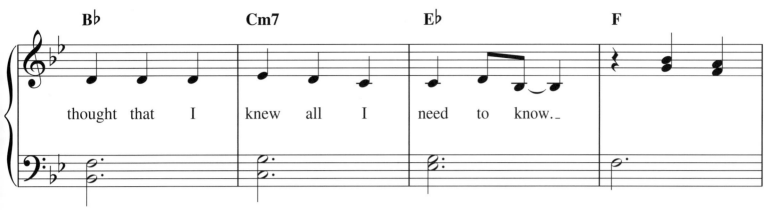

thought that I | knew all I | need to know.

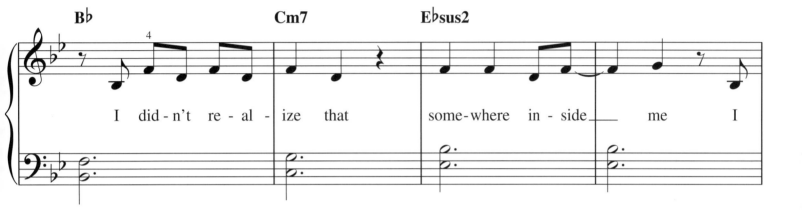

I did-n't re-al-ize that | some-where in-side me I

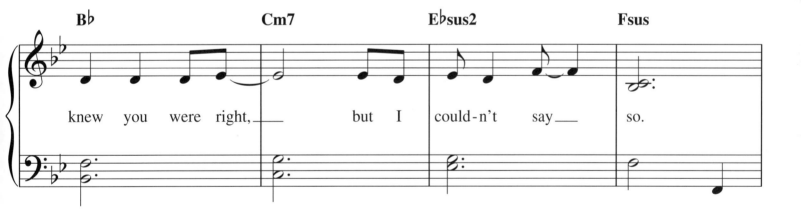

knew you were right, but I | could-n't say so.

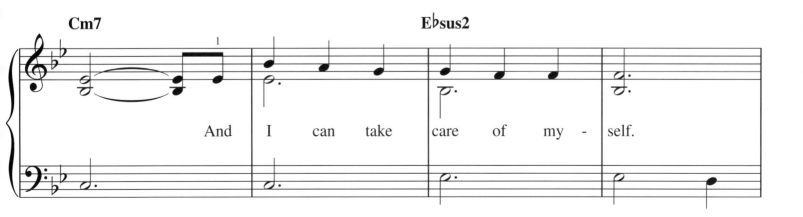

And I can take | care of my-self.

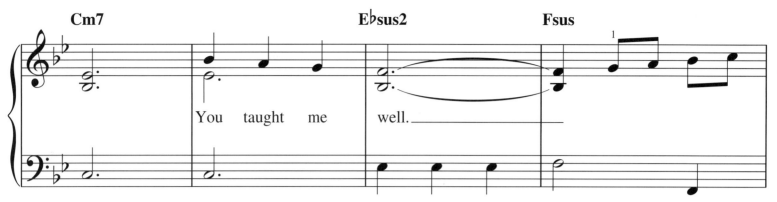

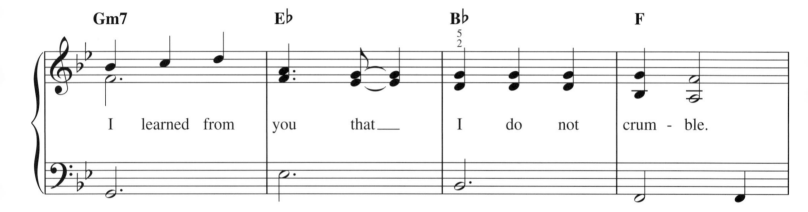

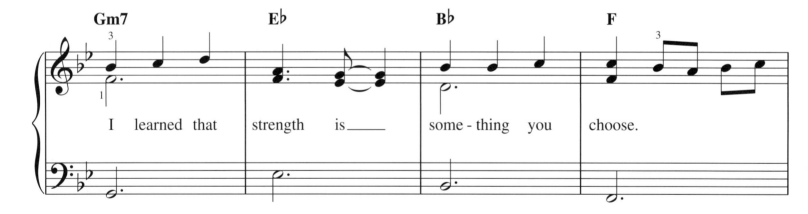

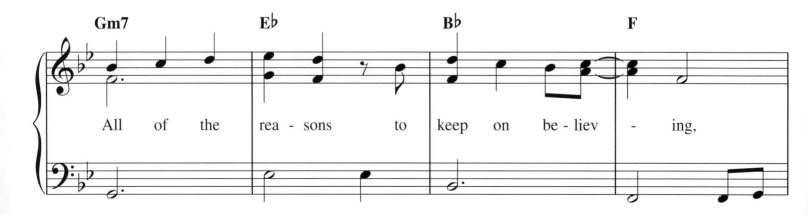

there's no ques - tion____ that's a les - son____ that I learned from

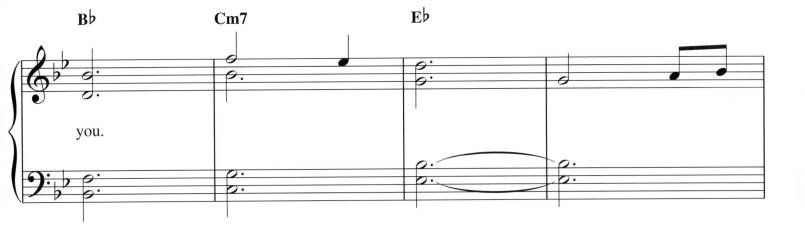

you.

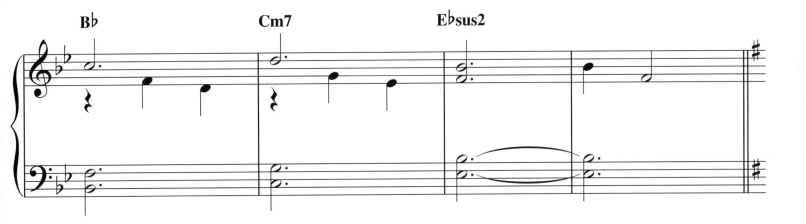

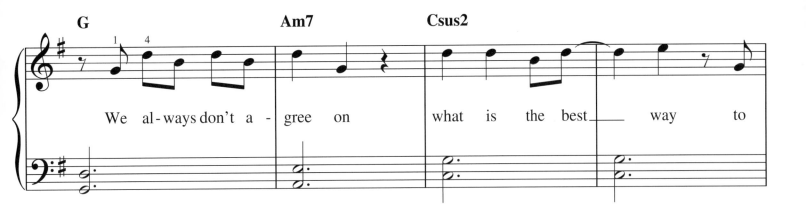

We al - ways don't a - gree on what is the best____ way to

get to the place____ that we're go - ing from____ here,

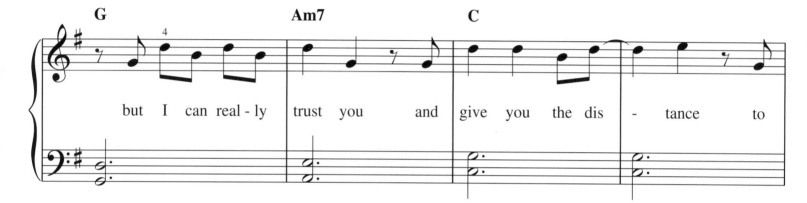

but I can real - ly trust you and give you the dis - tance to

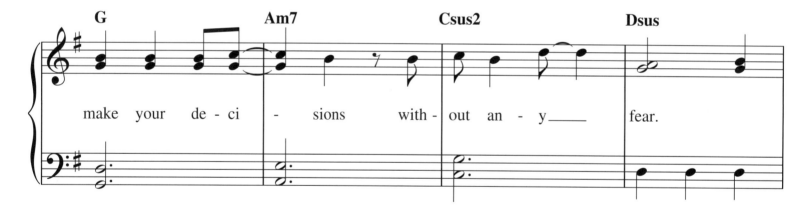

make your de - ci - sions with - out an - y____ fear.

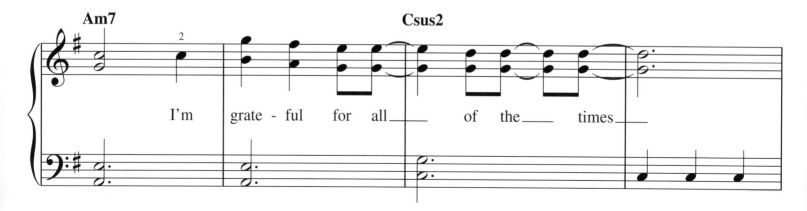

I'm grate - ful for all____ of the____ times____

69

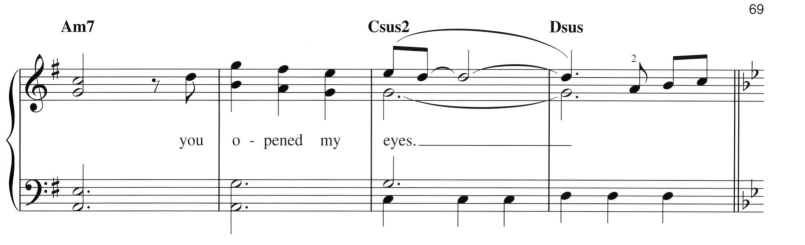

you o - pened my eyes._____

I learned from you that___ I do not___ crum - ble.

I learned that strength is___ some - thing you choose.

All of the rea - sons you keep on be - liev - ing,

To Coda

A♭

there's no ques-tion__ that's a les - son__ that I learned from

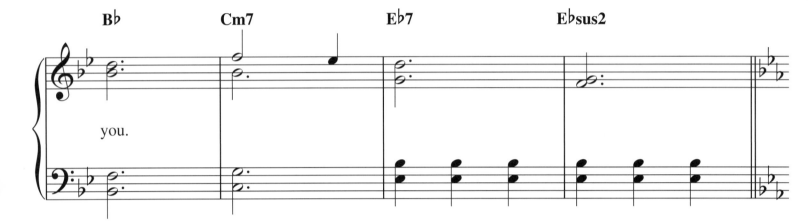

B♭   **Cm7**   **E♭7**   **E♭sus2**

you.

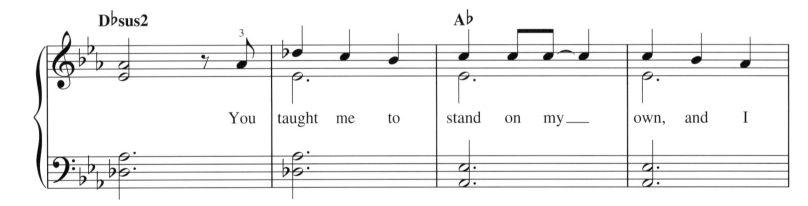

D♭sus2   **A♭**

You taught me to stand on my__ own, and I

E♭   **A♭/E♭ E♭**   **A♭/E♭ E♭**

thank you for that. It saved me, it made me.

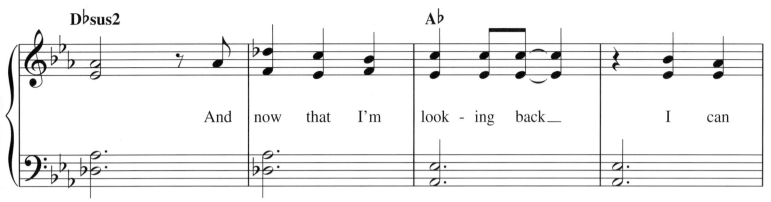

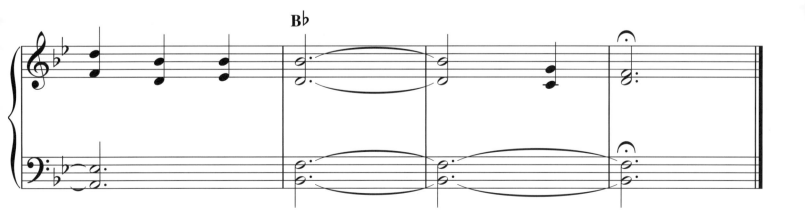

SHINING STAR

Words and Music by MAURICE WHITE,
PHILIP BAILEY and LARRY DUNN

Moderately

When you wish up-on___ a star (when you wish up-on___ a star), your

dreams will take you ver - y far, yeah, yeah, yeah, yeah.

When you wish up-on___ a dream (when you wish up-on___ a dream),

life ain't al - ways what it seems.

Once you see your light so clear, __

in the sky, so ver - y dear, _____ oh, ___ you're a

Asus   **Dsus**   **G**   **C**

shin - ing star, __ no mat - ter who you are, __ shin - ing

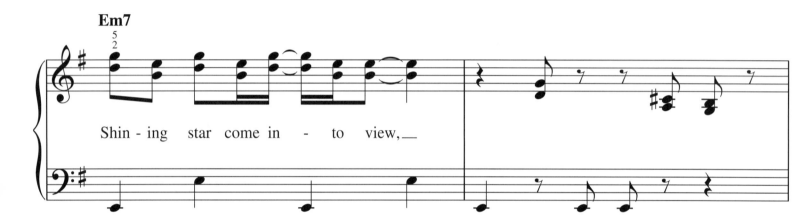

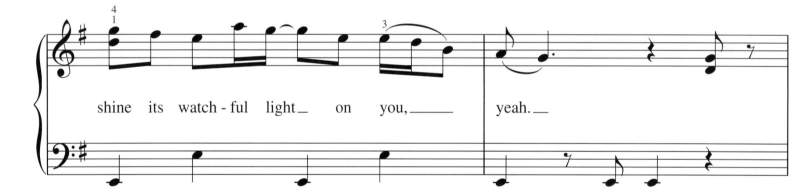

Be a child, you're free from sin.__ Be some-place, oh, yes, I can.__ You're a

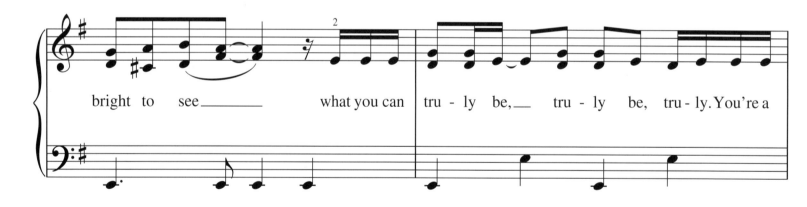

shin - ing star,__ no mat -ter who you are,_____ shin-ing

bright to see_____ what you can tru - ly be,__ tru - ly be, tru - ly. You're a

A7 **D7** **G7** **C7** **B♭7**

shin - ing star,__ no mat -ter who you are,__ shin-ing

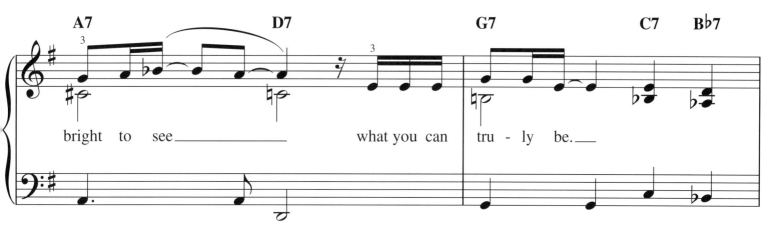

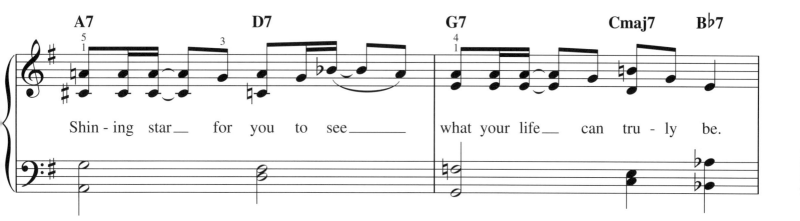

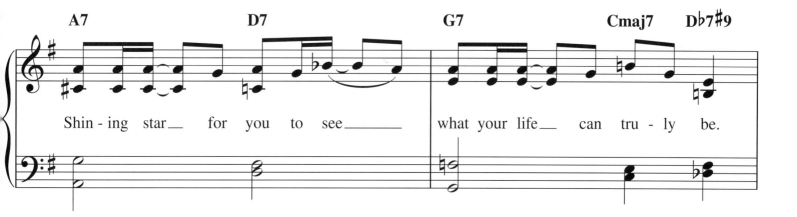